GRAHAM HOLDERNESS

Women in Love

Open University Press
Milton Keynes · Philadelphia

Open University Press
Open University Educational Enterprises Limited
12 Cofferidge Close
Stony Stratford
Milton Keynes MK11 1BY, England

and
242 Cherry Street
Philadelphia, PA 19106, USA

First published 1986

British Library Cataloguing in Publication Data

Holderness, Graham
  Women in love.—(Open guides to literature)
  1. Lawrence, D. H. Women in love
  I. Title   II. Lawrence, D. H.
  823'.912   PR6023.A93W65

ISBN 0–335–15254–6
ISBN 0–335–15253–8 Pbk

Library of Congress Cataloging in Publication Data

Holderness, Graham
  Women in love.
  (Open guides to literature)
  Bibliography: p.
  Includes index.
  1. Lawrence, D. H. (David Herbert), 1885–1930.
Women in love. I. Title. II. Series.
PR6023.A93W6535 1986   823'.912   86–768

ISBN 0–335–15254–6

ISBN 0–335–15253–8 (pbk.)

Text design by Clarke Williams
Typeset by S & S Press, Abingdon, Oxfordshire
Printed in Great Britain by J. W. Arrowsmith Ltd, Bristol

for Tristan, Tamsyn and Matthew

Contents

Series Editor's Preface

The intention of this series is to provide short introductory books about major writers, texts, and literary concepts for students of courses in Higher Education which substantially or wholly involve the study of Literature.

The series adopts a pedagogic approach and style similar to that of Open University material for Literature courses. *Open Guides* aim to inculcate the reading 'skills' which many introductory books in the field tend, mistakenly, to assume that the reader already possesses. They are, in this sense, 'teacherly' texts, planned and written in a manner which will develop in the reader the confidence to undertake further independent study of the topic. They are 'open' in two senses. First, they offer a three-way tutorial exchange between the writer of the *Guide*, the text or texts in question, and the reader. They invite readers to join in an exploratory discussion of texts, concentrating on their key aspects and on the main problems which readers, coming to the texts for the first time, are likely to encounter. The flow of a *Guide* 'discourse' is established by putting questions for the reader to follow up in a tentative and searching spirit, guided by the writer's comments, but not dominated by an over-arching and single-mindedly-pursued argument or evaluation, which itself requires to be 'read'.

Guides are also 'open' in a second sense. They assume that literary texts are 'plural', that there is no end to interpretation, and that it is for the reader to undertake the pleasurable task of discovering meaning and value in such texts. *Guides* seek to provide, in compact form, such relevant biographical, historical and cultural information as bears upon the reading of the text, and they point the reader to a selection of the best available critical discussions of it. They are not in themselves concerned to propose, or to counter, particular readings of the texts, but rather to put *Guide* readers in a position to do that for themselves. Experienced travellers learn to dispense with guides, and so it should be for readers of this series.

This *Open Guide* to D. H. Lawrence's *Women in Love* is best studied in conjunction with the Penguin English Library text of the novel, edited and with an introduction by Charles Ross (1982). Page references in the *Guide* are to this edition. Chapter references are also provided for the convenience of readers using a different edition. A definitive edition of the novel, edited by John Worthen and Lindeth Vasey as part of the Cambridge University Press collected works of Lawrence, is currently in preparation.

Graham Martin

Acknowledgements

Gratitude is due to the Series Editor, Graham Martin, for his formative comments and suggestions; to the students of the University College of Swansea Adult Education Department's Literature Foundation course, 1985–6, for their responsive interest in the book's methods and ideas; and to Louise Fleet for her accuracy and flexibility at the keyboard. Illustrations are reproduced by kind permission of Nottinghamshire County Library Service (p. 14); Nottingham University Library (pp. 13, 105 and 106); the South Wales Miners' Library (p. 115); and Tristan Holderness (p. 116).

1. Character, Narrative

Women in Love I–IV

Women in Love is widely regarded as the 'masterpiece' of a prolific, difficult, controversial, but persistently popular author. As such it has attracted a substantial body of criticism, and has formed the object of widely differing arguments and opinions. Controversy about the book's meaning and style is by no means closed or settled; though it is possible to categorize most of the critical writing into distinct 'schools' or 'camps'.

A study guide of this sort could not hope to offer a comprehensive reading of all the novel's artistic merits and problems, or to assist you with all the available secondary material; the aesthetic organization of *Women in Love* is too dense, the criticism too voluminous. What I hope to do in what follows is to offer a selective guide to the novel's most important features and difficulties, and to demonstrate the operations of criticism upon Lawrence's text. Once you have worked through the exercises and discussions I have provided, you should be in possession of the novel's central interests and problems, and in a position to engage yourself in the critical debate on its form and meaning.

Each chapter of the guide is organized around a group of Lawrence's chapters, so that you could conceivably work through it reading a section of the novel at a time: Lawrence's Chapters I–IV for my Chapter One, Chapters V–VIII for my Chapter Two, and so on. From Chapter Three of the guide onwards my concern with particular critical opinions (which are always of course based on an understanding of the whole novel) will make it more difficult for you to follow and participate in the arguments without a reading of the whole of Lawrence's text behind you. I would suggest that before tackling each of my Chapters One, Two and Three you should read those sections of the novel indicated at the head of each chapter; then read the rest of the novel straight through; and *re-read* the relevant passages of *Women in Love* for my Chapters Four, Five and Six.

   Women in Love is certainly not an easy book to read. When it was first published (in an American edition in 1920) it aroused a considerable amount of resistance, bafflement, hostility and anger, even from some of Lawrence's closest admirers. Although it has now been in circulation for over half a century and, since the 1950s, has been accepted by literary and educational establishments as a major classic, some of that initial difficulty still persists. Here are some examples of how the book aroused and provoked its first readers:

> The principal difficulty of the book is that it is difficult to read. It is full
> of absurdities; but Mr Lawrence, although he may occasionally repel
> by egotism, has at least the courage which leads him to risk absurdity
> for the sake of what he holds to be the truth. The difficulty is another
> matter. It arises from the static quality of the book, the lack of momen-
> tum. It arises also from the intrinsic similarity of all the characters.[1]

Those and similar charges have been echoed by many subsequent readers and students of the novel: it is difficult to read, full of absurdities, lacking in momentum, and fails to distinguish clearly between its characters. Another reviewer ironically addressed the latter allegation:

> The two heroines, Gudrun and Ursula, are almost as indistinguishable
> in character and conversation as they are in their amours and their clo-
> thing. They have innumerable pairs of stockings, which they change
> several times in one chapter. But no diversification of pink hat, blue
> stockings, orange jumper really distinguishes one from the other, and
> when towards the end of the feverish tale they both go abroad even the
> young men who accompany them – Birkin and Crich – lose their iden-
> tities and become one and the same young man.[2]

John Middleton Murry, writer, colleague and, for a time, a close friend of Lawrence's, added to these accusations of absurdity and. lack of distinctive characterization a third charge, that the book's style is monotonous, incantatory and obscure:

> *Women in Love* is five hundred pages of passionate vehemence, wave
> after wave of turgid, exasperated writing impelled towards some dis-
> tant and invisible end; the persistent underground beating of some
> dark and inaccessible sea in an underworld whose inhabitants are
> known by this alone, that they writhe continually, like the damned, in
> a frenzy of sexual awareness of one another. Their creator believes

that he can distinguish the writhing of one from the writhing of
another ... to him they are utterly and profoundly different; to us they
are all the same.[3]

Even F. R. Leavis, the critic whose pioneering essays subsequently
established Lawrence's status in the canon of 'classic' authors, wrote
in 1930 that the book was hard to read and the characters peculiarly
undiscriminated: 'to get through it calls for great determination ...
the characters tend to disintegrate into swirls of conflicting impulses
and emotions'.[4] Cruder contemporary reactions emphasized the element of 'absurdity', the 'peculiarity' of the characters, a view usually
associated with the intensity of their sexual experience: 'one would
have to sweep the world before getting together such a collection of
abnormalities'.[5] A reviewer in the reactionary magazine *John Bull*
stated forthrightly that 'most of his characters are obviously mad';
and that this madness evidently had something to do with sexuality:
'I do not claim to be a literary critic, but I know dirt when I smell it,
and here it is in heaps'.[6]

I would like you to begin your reading of *Women in Love* with
these opinions in mind. It is very unlikely that you will encounter
difficulties of such an extreme and intense kind: but the resistance
and hostilities of readers can be very instructive. Read the first five
chapters of the novel, thinking about the problems raised by these
criticisms, which can be isolated and listed like this:

1 The characters cannot be distinguished from one another.
2 The characters are peculiar, abnormal and absurd.
3 The novel is static, lacking momentum and narrative progress.
4 The style is passionate and vehement, but monotonous and
   obscure.
5 The novel overemphasizes the importance of sexual experience.

When you have completed this preparatory reading, work through
the following exercises and discussions, which are organized around
particular chapters of the novel.

Let us begin by looking carefully at how the novel presents its
principal characters. Please read Chapter I ('Sisters'), and make notes
on the following questions:

1 What impression are we given by the opening pages of Ursula and
   Gudrun Brangwen, and what narrative methods has the author
   employed to convey that impression – omniscient narrator, first-
   person narrative, subjective 'stream-of-consciousness'? Pay
   particular attention to the description of their walk through

Beldover (I.57–8). How does the novelist in that passage convey aspects of 'character' to the reader?

2 What information is given about the character of Gerald Crich (I.61–2)? What techniques of characterization are employed?

3 What impression do you receive of Hermione Roddice (I.62–4), and from whose viewpoint is the passage narrated?

4 What are we told of the character of Birkin himself?

DISCUSSION

1 The opening conversation between the sisters (I.53–7), employs a familiar novelistic technique, a mixture of description and dialogue, to convey aspects of character. The narrator is an anonymous, impersonal voice supplying descriptive detail of setting and appearances, and also offering some analytical comment and information about the subjective state of the characters; who in turn tell us about themselves by what the author gives them to say.

The initial situation would not be out of place in a Jane Austen novel: two young women sit in their father's house, one drawing, one embroidering, both talking about marriage. The dialogue and description employ familiar, conventional fictional techniques to tell us about the women's situation, and to distinguish between their characters. We learn that both are unhappy and frustrated at home, both seeking some escape from the boredom of their lives – Ursula is 'afraid at the depth of her feeling against the home . . .' (I.57). Both are preoccupied by, yet resistant to, the prospect of marriage. Both women are evidently approaching a critical moment of their lives when something decisive is likely to happen: 'The sisters found themselves confronted by a void, a terrifying chasm, as if they had looked over the edge' (I.57). Gudrun is distinguished from Ursula by physical appearance and by expression: her look of 'confidence and diffidence', contrasts with Ursula's 'sensitive expectancy' (I.57). So far, it is impossible to see anything in the novel's method that would cause even a reader of the 1920s to have difficulties of comprehension or acceptance.

Yet even here there are aspects of the writing which seem to take us to the edge of this familiarly 'normal' social milieu, and to the edge of this kind of realistic style and presentation. If that 'terrifying chasm' (I.57) glimpsed by Ursula and Gudrun were to become more than a figure of speech describing a person's anxiety about the future, if it became some dreadful apocalyptic event impending in the external world, it would obviously bring into this quiet suburban living-room a disturbing element of nightmare. The 'realistic' style tells us that both sisters are bored, frustrated and uncertain: but other touches of style tell us that they are *afraid*, without realistically providing any convincing explanation of the basis of that fear. Ursula, you may have noted, is afraid not of her situation, but of 'the depth of her feeling against' her ordinary life – 'home, milieu, atmosphere, condition'. Her social existence becomes strangely lifeless, unreal – 'this obsolete life' – while the fear, located within the mind of a character alienated and estranged from the familiar, the everyday, the 'normal', becomes more alive, present and real.

The description of their walk through Beldover intensifies this more disturbing quality of the writing. Re-read the description on pp. 57–8, beginning 'The two girls were soon walking swiftly', to 'children called out names'. Did you notice that the narrative voice is sometimes 'authorial', but sometimes that of a character? The authorial voice describes a mixed social setting of industrial and agricultural activities, collieries and cornfields. The perspective is not a single-dimensional one: the landscape is 'dark, soiled', but columns of smoke appear 'magic within the dark air' (I.58). A little later (I.59) the same voice talks of a 'glamour of blackness', which seems 'darkly to gleam in the air'. The authorial consciousness is aware of diversity and difference, brightness and darkness; and the characteristic human presence in the landscape seems connected with both:

> The path on which the sisters walked was black, trodden-in by the feet of the recurrent colliers . . . the stile that led again into the road was rubbed shiny by the moleskins of the passing miners.   (I.58)

The two sentences are syntactically similar, and balanced in a poetic contrast: the miners 'tread in' the ubiquitous blackness, and yet their passage can produce reflected light.

Gudrun's version of the landscape is quite different: for her there is no such diversity, but a world transformed into an 'underworld': what she sees is not a real world, but its 'replica', a soiled landscape of nightmare peopled by the living dead. The experience of looking at it is 'like being mad' (I.58). Gudrun's description seems to project the 'void' of the anxious imagination onto the external world itself. Is she describing her surroundings, or the contents of her mind? There seems, for a start, to be a clear difference between the authorial voice of the third paragraph, and Gudrun's own description of the mining landscape.

But the first paragraph seems to contain a mingling of the authorial voice and the voice of Gudrun's consciousness: an apparently impersonal narrator talks of the town as 'utterly formless and sordid', of its 'amorphous ugliness'; while the character's consciousness registers impressions in the same language: 'Yet forward she went, through the whole *sordid* gamut of pettiness, the long *amorphous*, gritty street . . . this *shapeless*, barren *ugliness*' (I.57, my italics). The difficulty of distinguishing the authorial voice from the inner voice of the character, can be seen very clearly in the passage of prose preceding Gudrun's spoken comments: which begins as authorial narrative, 'They turned off the main road . . .' but ends with observations which are obviously Gudrun's: 'No one was ashamed of it all' (I.57). The authorial and the character-consciousness seem to bleed into each other, making it impossible to separate them, and causing serious difficulties of interpretation. How do we know whether the 'madness' Gudrun speaks of is what we normally think of as madness – the insane mind bending the external world to accord with its own distorted vision; or is that external world, as Gudrun says, so alienated and inhuman that it colours the mind itself with madness?

2   What of the 'characterization' of Gerald Crich (I.61–2)? Surely it offers very little information of the usual 'character' type. One sentence describes his physical appearance; then the focus is shifted immediately to stranger, more elusive qualities which distinguish him not only from the people around, but from human kind itself: 'as if he did not belong to the same creation as the people about him' (I.61). Gerald is further dehumanized by the foregrounding of metaphors which actually replace the physical being, the social man. That 'exaggeratedly well-dressed' figure 'rather above middle height' recedes: and for his presence is substituted a composite image-complex combining associations of the arctic north, brightness and cold, and the untamed beauty of the wolf. The 'author' of this 'description' is not the novelist's narrative persona: here one central character, Gerald, is mediated to the reader entirely through the consciousness of another, Gudrun. The sentence 'Gudrun lighted on him at once' signals to the reader that this poetic fantasy is an articulation of her response to him. The situation, one in which a woman sees a man and is attracted to him, is surely very familiar from many kinds of fiction: there is nothing unusual about Gudrun's assertion: 'I shall know more of that man'. The experience itself however is expressed in far stranger language:

> 'His totem is the wolf', she repeated to herself. 'His mother is an old, unbroken wolf'. And then she experienced a keen paroxysm, a transport, as if she had made some incredible discovery, known to nobody else on earth. A strange transport took possession of her, all her veins were in a paroxysm of violent sensation.   (I.61)

In Gudrun's strange fantastic vision Gerald's 'totem' (hereditary emblem of the tribe or clan to which he belongs) is the wolf. By introducing the idea of 'totem', a ritual symbol of magical powers, Gudrun is not simply *comparing* Gerald with a wolf, but affirming the kind of intimate relationship between human beings and sacred animals possible only in a primitive tribal culture. The emphasis is confirmed by the metaphorical assertion that his mother *is* a wolf. Having spoken those words, almost a kind of ritual incantation, Gudrun experiences a sexual/religious 'transport' or ecstasy in which she apprehends an apparently non-human power. She feels that both she and Gerald are estranged from the everyday world, brought into communion on some plane of fantasy: '. . . is there really some pale, gold, arctic light that envelopes only us two?' (I.62).

The suggestions of ritual and myth offered here will be discussed further in Chapter Five. Meanwhile, I would like you to consider a passage in which Lawrence himself spoke of his methods of 'characterization'. The context is a letter Lawrence wrote in 1914 while writing a projected novel which was later split into *The Rainbow* and *Women in Love*. Edward Garnett had evidently criticized the draft on the grounds of false characterization and poor 'psychology'. Lawrence's reply was that he was working to a new conception of 'psychology'. (The language of this passage is occasionally technical and difficult, as Lawrence was temporarily using a quasi-scientific vocabulary drawn from the work of the Italian Futurists.)

> I don't think the psychology is wrong: it is only that I have a different attitude to my characters, and that necessitates a different attitude in you . . . that which is physic – non-human, in humanity, is more interesting to me than the old-fashioned human element – which causes one to conceive a character in a certain moral scheme and make him consistent . . . You mustn't look in my novel for the old stable ego of the character. There is another ego, according to whose action the individual is unrecognizable, and passes through, as it were, allotropic states which it needs a deeper sense than any we've been used to exercise, to discover are states of the same single radically-unchanged element (like as diamond and coal are the same pure single element of carbon. The ordinary novel would trace the history of the diamond – but I say, 'Diamond, what! This is carbon.' And my diamond might be coal or soot, and my theme is carbon). Again I say, don't look for the development of the novel to follow the lines of certain characters: the characters fall into the form of some other rhythmic form, like when one draws a fiddle bow across a fine tray delicately sanded, the sand takes lines unknown.[7]

'Physic' means 'physiological'; 'allotropic' refers to substances which can exhibit different physical properties while remaining fundamentally unchanged. Study this passage carefully. Does this new conception of 'psychology' help to elucidate the characterization of

Gerald? Gudrun certainly seems, like the author himself, less interested in what Gerald is in terms of the 'old-fashioned human element', and more interested in his 'non-human' properties. Gerald the social individual is momentarily transformed, for her, into the primitive being bearing the emblem of the wolf. The 'old stable ego of the character' disintegrates as the person mutates into different forms.

3   The description of Hermione, by contrast, is quite different from that of Gerald. There is a great deal more physical description of Hermione's dress and appearance; there is much more contextual detail about her social status, connections and activities. Most of this information is registered by Ursula's perceiving consciousness: the description begins 'Ursula watched them come up the steps' (I.62); and later reminds the reader of who is perceiving Hermione: 'Ursula watched her with fascination' (I.62). As Gudrun is to become Gerald's lover, and Ursula is to see Hermione as a rival for Birkin's affection, there are perhaps good reasons for using these different narrative techniques. Nonetheless, they produce very different 'characterizations': the figure of Gerald displaced from social reality into realms of myth and fantasy; that of Hermione located firmly within a social milieu and its intellectual ambience.

The focus shifts with the paragraph beginning 'She had various intimacies . . .' (I.63) to Gudrun's point of view: 'It would be queer to meet again . . .' seems an utterance from Gudrun's angle of vision. The passage then modulates into a form of interior monologue in which Hermione's own consciousness is reporting on her experience: 'Hermione *knew herself* to be well-dressed . . .'. The subsequent passage dealing with Hermione's desire for immunity from 'the world's judgement', and her secret vulnerability, is all internalized, all the stream of her own consciousness. At least one sentence seems to offer a judgement from a more detached, external perspective: 'And all the while the pensive, tortured woman piled up her own defences of aesthetic knowledge, and culture, and world-visions, and disinterestedness' (I.64). That is not, surely, the character's own judgement. Is it the author's? Perhaps: though the subject of that particular paragraph is Birkin; and its critical accent anticipates Birkin's own critique of Hermione (see *Women in Love*, III.91–3; discussed below, pp. 16–18).

4   The description of Birkin appears to be from Ursula's point-of-view: it is framed by the observations 'And then Ursula noticed again . . .' (I.67) and 'Ursula was left thinking about Birkin' (I.68). Yet the passage reads more like authorial comment, with its neatly-balanced judgement of great perceptiveness and insight: Birkin's ostensible 'ordinariness' diagnosed as a defensive strategy, his apparent 'ease'

the skill of a social tightrope-walker. Presently (I.68) the sisters discuss the same topic: but the effect is different. There is surely some authorial irony in their sense of pique and injured pride, because Birkin doesn't single *them* out as deserving of special interest and consideration. Either the character sketch of Birkin is the narrator's, or Ursula responds to him there at a deeper level than the attention she gives to Gudrun's comments.

Let us try to draw some conclusions from these different methods of presenting 'character'. One point emerges clearly: that it is particularly difficult, in the case of *this* novel, to talk about 'character' without also talking about other things: narrative, point-of-view, mythical allusions, 'allotropic states' of the changing individual. We seem to be presented here with something different from the conventional 'division of labour' between narrator and characters, where the two occupy discrete spaces and speak different languages. We have found in the space of one chapter examples of impersonal narration, dramatized dialogue, interior monologue, and character-description rendered from the viewpoint of another character. Not only do these different techniques co-exist, within the same chapter, they continually flow into one another in a fluid, unstable relationship. The result is disturbing and disorientating, since the world of the novel is not mapped out with any reassuring clarity and precision. The narrator is not a reliable personal acquaintance communicating necessary information, staking out the moral perimeters and guiding the reader's judgement. The characters are not passively subdued to a controlling authorial consciousness: they have the power to transform the world into a mirror of their own subjective experience. The characters are not consistent, stable egos but volatile foci of energy capable of transformation into new forms.

Below are three extracts from critical essays on this theory of character. Read and compare them, writing notes on what seem to you their important differences, and on whether they can help to illuminate your reading of the novel so far.

(a)   ... Lawrence had to insist on those mysterious forces of otherness which are scattered without, and darkly concentrated within, the body and mind of man. He had to, even though, by doing so, he imposed upon himself, as a writer of novels, a very serious handicap. For according to his view of things most of men's activities were more or less criminal distractions from the proper business of human living ... But as though this drastic limitation of his subject were not sufficient, he went still further and, in some of his novels, refused even to write of human personalities in the accepted sense of the term ... Hence the strangeness of his novels; and hence also, it must be admitted, certain qualities of violent

monotony and intense indistinctness, qualities which make some
of them, for all their richness and their unexpected beauty, so
curiously difficult to get through. Most of us are more interested
in diamond and coal than in undifferentiated carbon, however
vividly described.   (Aldous Huxley, 1932)[8]

(b)   Conventional   characterization   of   the   sort   employed   in
nineteenth-century novels, or, for that matter, in *Sons and Lovers*, was felt to be inadequate . . . the abandonment of the 'certain
moral scheme' means that a character is judged not by social or
by ethical criteria but by the degree to which he is true to his
deepest being, to the 'carbon' of his nature. The conception of
character as a series of 'allotropic states' is based, it seems to me,
on profound psychological truth . . :   (H. M. Daleski, 1965)[9]

(c)   As an artist interested in 'profound intuitions of life', and in inhuman elements of the human person, which together imply a radical revision of traditional moral ideas, he cannot afford to waste
time on the portrayal of individuals possessing a conventional
social, moral and psychological character within a 'certain moral
scheme' . . . The difficulty with these ideas as they apply to any
novel – although the same difficulties might not present themselves in a ballet, musical composition, or painting concerned
with ultimates of being – should be obvious. In all narrative art,
existence must grapple with and help to define essence; if one
cares to differentiate characters from one another . . . it must be
done in terms of what they do, think and feel humanly and
socially, and these terms must mediate what they 'inhumanly'
are. A representation of sheer 'isness' would make it impossible
to distinguish one character from another, and all the characters
from undifferentiated life itself. If the essence of a character is carbon, then the essence of all characters is carbon, and you cannot
write a novel about carbon and nothing but carbon.   (Julian
Moynahan, 1963)[10]

DISCUSSION

Extracts (a) and (c) are in many ways similar, are they not? Let us first
consider extract (b). Daleski contrasts 'conventional characterization' such as we find in the nineteenth-century novel, or in Lawrence's own earlier productions, with the 'profound psychological
truth' of this concern with 'deepest being'. For this critic, the
emphasis on 'essence' rather than 'existence' – on some central core
of an individual's externally observable behaviour, objective characteristics and social relations – is a positive achievement, taking the
novel closer to the reality of human experience. Daleski doesn't
acknowledge, as the other two critics do, that this 'essentialist'
approach to character might raise serious difficulties for a writer of

narrative fiction. He also assumes, perhaps without sufficient warrant, that the novelist was declaring an interest in the 'carbon' of human nature to the exclusion of the varying forms that element may adopt. Lawrence's metaphor doesn't, after all, imply a refusal to admit the existence of 'diamond' and 'coal': it only suggests that he is probing towards a new awareness of their common structural unity.

The other two extracts emphasize rather the problems invited by this new view of character. Aldous Huxley suggested that the reduction of character to its elements embraces a 'serious handicap': most readers are more interested in the variable forms of human existence than in the immutable structure of human essence. Where Daleski referred critically to 'conventional characterization', Huxley testifies to a reluctance to abandon 'the accepted sense of the term' human personality. In Huxley's view the consequences of this emphasis of Lawrence's were those very qualities of difficulty, monotony, obscurity, and undifferentiated characterization perceived by many of the novel's early readers.

Aldous Huxley, of course, *was* one of those early readers: but Julian Moynahan, writing in 1963, took much the same view. *Narrative* and *dramatic* art (which he distinguishes from other, less representational cultural forms) can't afford to separate 'existence' from 'essence': what people *are* must be mediated to the reader through a representation of what they *do*: the human, ethical and social dimensions can't be dropped without subverting the form of the novel. Moynahan's conclusion is, in fact, that Lawrence managed to hold the two co-ordinates of character ('existence' and 'essence') together; he didn't consider the possibility that Lawrence might have *wanted* to subvert the traditional forms of narrative fiction with his revolutionary methods (this view will be considered again in subsequent chapters; see, e.g. pp. 82–4 below).

These echoes of the initial resistances of contemporary readers will perhaps suggest that the novel's difficulties cannot be explained entirely in terms of fictional fashions. Perhaps Lawrence's method of characterization was founded on a contradiction: was he creating traditional 'characters' on the basis of a belief that traditional 'character' didn't really exist? Furthermore, it is possible that the concept of 'character' is inseparable from the concept of a 'certain moral scheme'. A 'character' is an individual possessing certain features of personality, certain capacities for change and development, and a certain orientation within the world of society. But if a character possesses this kind of consistency, does that not imply a consistent point-of-view from which the character is regarded; which in turn

implies a consistent ideology or ethical stance? If the consistent viewpoint is abandoned along with the consistent moral scheme, what
happens to the idea of a consistent character, 'the old, stable ego'?

Lawrence's use of the term 'ego' links his thinking with that of
Freud. Lawrence absorbed some Freudian ideas from Frieda
(Weekly, neé Von Richthofen, whom he met in 1912 and married in
1914) and her sister Else, a member of an advanced intellectual
circle in Germany, and to whom *The Rainbow* was dedicated. In
1912 Lawrence wrote in a letter an explanatory account of *Sons and
Lovers* which bears obvious Freudian influence.[11]

We have seen from our reading of the first chapter of *Women in
Love* that there is certainly no consistency of *viewpoint*; 'character'
can be rendered from an authorial viewpoint, from the perspective of
another character, or by interior monologue. The effect of this shifting narrative perspective is to undermine the reader's confidence in
any 'certain moral scheme'. Nor is there any sense of the character as
a constant bundle of characteristics constrained within binding
parameters. The narrative method seems to produce striking contradictions of character: Gerald is simultaneously a well-dressed
coal-owner's son and 'a good-humoured, smiling wolf'; Hermione
presents an impressively poised appearance to conceal an inner chaos
of anxiety; Birkin is both a model of natural affability and a man
walking a psychological tightrope. But is it actually the case that
Lawrence concentrates on 'deeper being' to the exclusion of human
and social behaviour? Isn't the relationship between 'existence' and
'essence', what one *is* and what one *does*, still preserved, though seen
as very complex, changing and often contradictory? Lawrence seems
more concerned to explore the complex relations between the elements of human personality and the way those elements are expressed in social behaviour and interpersonal relationships, than with
abandoning all interest in 'existence' in favour of an exclusive con-
centration on 'essence'.

We can now turn directly to methods of narration. Please read
Chapter II of *Women in Love* ('Shortlands') and make some notes on
these methods. Is this chapter, like Chapter I, constructed from an
amalgamation of several viewpoints: or is a more consistent narrative perspective sustained?

DISCUSSION

Compared with Chapter I, 'Shortlands' seems relatively straightforward in its narrative technique. The chapter begins by establishing
clear temporal and spatial links with the previous chapter: an

D. H. Lawrence in 1913
'his nature was clever and separate . . .'
Women in Love, I.67

Lamb Close House
'*a long, low old house, a sort of manor farm . . .*'
Women in Love, II.71

account of a wedding-party will follow the previous description of the ceremony; and the scene has shifted from Willey Green to Short-lands: 'The Brangwens went home to Beldover, the wedding party gathered at Shortlands, the Criches' home' (II.71). The voice there is that of an authorial narrative persona who describes, records and comments: 'The scene was rural and picturesque, very peaceful, and the house had a charm of its own' (II.71). This omniscient narrator records the whole episode with an impersonal, objective attention: some of the descriptions resemble the vision of a stationary film cam-era: 'There was a great rustling of skirts, swift glimpses of smartly-dressed women, a child danced through the hall and back again, a maid-servant came and went hurriedly' (II.71). The perceiving con-sciousness here records only what passes before it: neither moving nor responding. The same omniscient narrator rounds the chapter off, by giving us a privileged access to the feelings of the characters, Birkin and Gerald: 'They burned with each other, inwardly. This they would never admit' (II.83). As readers we are given access to an awareness beyond the conscious reach of the characters themselves, an awareness recorded by an anonymous, independent, omniscient witness.

Parts of the chapter, however, are concerned with one character, Birkin: and some passages reflect the interior motions of Birkin's mind. 'Then he remembered with a slight shock, that that was Cain's cry. And Gerald was Cain, if anybody' (II.74). Birkin, you will observe, thinks about Gerald in mythological terms rather than in the context of the social milieu: not as a member of the British *haute bourgeoisie*, but as a protagonist in the Old Testament fratricidal fable. Again, there is nothing unusual in this combination of an objective narrative perspective and an emphasis on the experience of one character: it is a familiar fictional convention (common in, for exam-ple, Jane Austen). Perhaps the only difficulty raised by this chapter is its being so *unlike* the first: though clearly linked in space and time, the two chapters seem stylistically out of touch with each other.

Look again at those passages dealing with Birkin's experience of this event, especially pp. 72–4, 79, 81–2. Is there a difference be-tween the view we get from the impersonal narrative, and the attitudes conveyed by Birkin's point-of-view?

DISCUSSION

The impersonal narrative descriptions seem concerned to constitute the scene as a pleasant and orderly social ritual in the familiar fictional scene of a country house (the chapter heading 'Shortlands' may even recall the many nineteenth-century novels named after such places). The scene and the style seem appropriate to each other. From the first page of the chapter we can isolate a list of words which accumulate to compose a familiar setting, a successful enactment of the traditional code of gentry hospitality: 'rural, picturesque, peaceful, charm, homely, friendly, hospitality, calm, genial, happy' (II.71).

Within this narrative setting however, Birkin feels an outsider: 'Yet he was tense, feeling that he and the elderly, estranged woman were conferring together, like traitors, like enemies within the camp of the other people' (II.72). The emphasis of the opening paragraphs is all on *pleasure* and *hospitality*: the narrative invites the reader to participate in a familiar fictional pleasure, just as the Crich house opens its doors to a sociable gathering of welcomed guests. Birkin's statements clash hard against this atmosphere of affability: 'People don't really matter ... It would be much better if they were just wiped out' (II.73). In contradiction then to a relatively conventional narrative style which emphasizes harmony, social unity and pleasure, the view of the individual is estranged, hostile and misanthropic. Instead of a decorous balance of authorial and character-perspectives, we find a relationship of contradiction: the individual is not at ease with society but alienated within it. Everything Birkin says and thinks in this chapter emanates from this alienated position: his alliance with the 'estranged' Mrs Crich (II.72–3), his misanthropy (II.73), his preoccupation with the death of Gerald's brother (II.74), his draining of the champagne glass (II.79), his strange ideas about spontaneity and aggression (II.82).

Read Chapter III ('Class-Room'), and make notes on the following questions:

1   What is the point of the chapter-heading 'Class-Room'? Does the class-room setting signify anything important?
2   The chapter makes several references to the hazel catkins. How do the catkins function in the narrative?
3   Examine the passage describing Ursula's response to Birkin's 'attractiveness' (III.94) – 'Ursula was watching him . . . did not relax'. Is this 'attractiveness' appreciated by the reader?

DISCUSSION

1   As Ursula is a teacher and Birkin an Inspector, the class-room is a natural location for them to meet. And yet the setting seems to have little literal or dramatic significance. Although the opening paragraphs invoke a very vivid picture of the school-room, the children

themselves remain shadowy presences, and the characters' occupations are given no prominence. The class-room becomes a setting in fact for a different kind of educational process: the bitter quarrel between Birkin and Hermione, which is fought out through a philosophical debate, and which clearly marks a decisive stage both in their relationship and in Ursula's personal development. 'Ursula was concerned now only with solving her own problems, in the light of his words' (III.92). The educator herself must be educated. When Birkin tries to protract the argument only to find the women united against him in jeering hostility, his assumption of pedagogic authority is ironically undermined: 'He sounded as if he were addressing a meeting' (III.94). 'Class-Room' seems to have more metaphorical than literal significance.

2   The hazel catkins, which are initially the objects of study in a botany lesson, become somethng like a controlling metaphor in the chapter. The vitality of the plant articulates the awakening emotions of the people:

> Birkin turned curiously to look at Ursula. Her eyes were round and wondering, bewildered, her mouth quivered slightly. She looked like one who is suddenly wakened . . . There was a living, tender beauty, like a tender light of dawn shining from her face. He looked at her with a new pleasure, feeling gay in his heart, irresponsible . . . 'The red ones, too!' he said, looking at the *flickers* of crimson that came from the *female bud* . . .
> . . . her heart quickened at the *flicker* of his voice.   (III.85; my italics).

Thus when Birkin requires Ursula to look at the catkins in a different way to perceive the essence of their sexuality (III.85–6), our attention is being focused on the quickening of their relationship as well as on the reproductive system of plants. Hermione uses the catkins as a pretext for an affected rapture of sensuous ecstasy (III.87); and they become the catalyst for the argument about spontaneity and consciousness (see below, Chapter Two, 'Ideas', for further discussion of the concepts involved in that argument). The physical object, the catkins, is there less for its literal function in a dramatized event, more for its possibilities of association and suggestion in a complex metaphorical structure. The catkins are used like an image in a poem: more for what they can be made to mean than for what they *are*. The chapter itself could be said to resemble a poem: organized around a controlling metaphor which does not recur elsewhere in the novel. Again, the technique of the single chapter operates to separate it from other contingent chapters.

3   The passage describing Birkin's 'physical attractiveness' (III.94) must come, surely, as something of a shock to the reader? The

impression we have been given in the preceding pages is utterly
unlike the 'attractiveness' Ursula sees: 'A dark flash went over his
face, a silent fury. He was hollow-cheeked and pale, almost
unearthly' (III.89); 'His voice was brutal, scornful, cruel' (III.89);
'He looked at her in mingled hate and contempt, also in pain because
she suffered, and in shame because he knew he tortured her . . . But
a bitterer red anger burned up to fury in him' (III.92). It is difficult to
conceive that what Ursula sees as 'attractiveness' in Birkin appears as
a result of some psychological *change* in the character. The image she
sees *co-exists* with the figure of brutal anger and bitter scorn. A
number of words and phrases suggest that Ursula is seeing something
'hidden' – 'another voice', 'another knowledge', 'invisible'; 'she
could not say what it was' (III.94). Birkin seems literally to be two
people: not the same man seen alternately by Hermione and
Ursula; but one man capable of expressing either of these two discrete personalities. In his relationship with Hermione he is one thing;
in his nascent relationship with Ursula, another.

  Read Chapter IV ('Diver') and make notes on the following
questions:

1 What seems to be the main concern of this chapter, and what is
   its primary *function* in the novel? Would you say that function
   was adequately defined by the chapter-heading, 'Diver'?
2 The first paragraph is a poetic evocation of natural energies, a
   celebration of natural 'creation'. Does this imagery recur in the
   chapter?
3 The descriptions of Gerald swimming also contain poetic evoca-
   tions of natural objects. Is the style of these passages similar to
   that of the opening paragraph, or quite different in its effects?

DISCUSSION

1 The apparition of Gerald diving into the pool is the only real
'event' of any consequence in the whole chapter. The sisters see the
Shortlands house, and meet with Hermione; but these incidents are
little more than a pretext for the topics of their conversation. The title
'Diver' thus focuses our attention onto a single distinctive event,
which yet doesn't seem to have any very obvious *literal* significance
in the chapter as a whole.

  The main preoccupation of the chapter seems to be with the sisters themselves, their different reactions, opinions and attitudes:
specifically with the gaps of understanding and conflicts of opinion
which occur over Gudrun's view of masculine liberty (IV.98);

Gerald's killing of his brother (IV.100); Hermione's alleged 'impudence' (IV.101); and the fashion for 'ordinariness' (IV.102). 'The two sisters were like a pair of scissors, snipping off everything that came athwart them; or like a knife and whetstone, the one sharpened against the other' (IV.101). That authorial comment seems to suggest that the sisters perform mutually compatible roles in a reciprocal, balanced relationship of creative conflict: evidently that is one way of 'reading' or interpreting their disagreements. There are other suggestions in the chapter that emphasize profound differences between the sisters, which the novel will perhaps go on to elaborate and refine.

2   The opening paragraph uses the springtime growth of plants and flowers as images of an awakening 'creation' in the natural world: 'The earth would be quickening and hastening in growth . . . the morning was full of a new creation' (IV.96).The image of growing plants recurs at the end of the chapter, where it is associated with Ursula: 'Her spirit was active, her life like a shoot that is growing steadily, but which has not yet come above ground' (IV.103).

3   When Gerald first appears, leaping into vision with a startling precipitance, he too seems to represent 'a new creation': 'Suddenly, from the boat-house, a white figure ran out, frightening in its swift sharp transit, across the old landing-stage . . . Thè whole otherworld wet and remote, he had to himself. He could move into the pure translucency of the grey, uncreated water' (IV.96). The water itself is 'uncreated': but the swimmer occupies and appropriates its neutrality to his own distinctive gesture and motion: 'The sisters stood watching the swimmer move further into the grey, moist, full space of the water, pulsing with his own small, invading motion, and arched over with mist and dim woods' (IV.97).

The descriptive passages that follow introduce a different note, as we observe Gudrun's reaction to the swimmer, and Gerald's response to the experience of being observed. He is filled with a pride of power, superiority and exultation; she with a sense of envy, desire and inconsolable loss:

> And she stood motionless gazing over the water at the face which washed up and down on the flood, as he swam steadily. From his separate element he saw them and he exulted to himself because of his own advantage, his possession of a world to himself. He was immune and perfect . . . He exulted in his isolation in the new element, unquestioned and unconditional. He was happy, thrusting with his legs and all his body, without bond or connection anywhere, just himself of the watery world.

Gudrun envied him almost painfully. Even this momentary possession of pure isolation and fluidity seemed to her so terribly desirable that she felt herself as if damned, out there on the high road.
(IV.97–8)

This desire of the individual to become a purely isolated, relationless
unit independent of all human and social connection is common to
both Gudrun and Gerald; the formidable energy expended in a voyage to nowhere is characteristically Gerald's: 'Where does his 'go' go
to?' (IV.99). The intensity and significance of Gudrun's emotion is
suggested by the strong language ('as if damned') and the fact that
Ursula seems to feel her sister's outburst about masculine freedom is
not really the point. The idea of individual isolation is developed
throughout the novel, and towards the end emerges as a dominant
characteristic, certainly of these two characters, perhaps of all 'significant' individuals in this society (see below, pp. 120–4).

Does this distinction between the sisters prefigure their ultimate
fates? In 'Diver' it is Gudrun who feels drawn towards the kind of
pure isolation and perfect self-sufficiency symbolized by Gerald's
'possession of a world to himself' in the water; and Ursula is, by contrast, related to that imagery of springtime growth and quickening
life which perhaps signifies genuine possibilities of creative individual development. When Gudrun declares a creed of violent misanthropy ('Of course, the only thing to do is to depise them all – just all'
– IV.102) she simultaneously feels a 'queer, uncertain envy and dislike' of Ursula. Perhaps we have here the beginnings of a large moral
distinction between the sisters which will lead Gudrun to a tragic
consummation, and Ursula to creative growth and fulfilment.

Some interpretations of the novel, which will be discussed in
Chapter Three, regard this desire for isolation as a kind of psychological sickness, one of the symptomatic *malaises* of modern civilization: to which Gudrun and Gerald succumb, while Birkin and Ursula
resist. As you will see when we come to discuss these matters in
Chapter Three, the distinction is by no means so absolute: the desire
for 'singleness' is felt and articulated by no one so emphatically as
Birkin; and the desire to shed relationships and connections, to
become autonomous and free, is declared most explicitly by Ursula
(see Chapters XIII, and XXIX, pp.481–2). We cannot proceed any
further with these problems without considering the novel's employment of intellectual ideas, and the relationship of these with Lawrence's own 'philosophy'.

To sum up what we have gathered about narrative from our
reading of these early chapters: it is initially evident that where Lawrence uses conventional narrative techniques (as in the opening of

'Shortlands') he does so with unorthodox intentions; since the easy going familiarity of the omniscient Victorian-style narrator is challenged by the contemptuous alienation of his principal character. Both voices are, in a sense, the author's: but the relationship between them is one of contradiction. Chapters are not linked sequentially or in terms of a gradually-developing 'plot'; instead the author uses an episodic technique, with chapters tending to adopt their own individual shapes around central controlling metaphors. Often 'incidents' or events, the key features of a traditional narrative, do not contain the important meanings of the story; we have to look elsewhere for them, in subjective experiences, personal relationships, the perspectives of disengaged and alienated individuals.

If you want to pursue these thoughts about narrative further on your own, I suggest that you consider the methods used in Chapters VI–VII, which describe with the utmost vividness Gerald's affair with a woman who will not figure in the novel again; if we expected Pussum (the name was changed to 'Minette' as a consequence of a libel threat) to figure again in the novel, the expectation would be disappointed. She reappears only very briefly in Chapter XXVIII. Notice also in this group of chapters the title 'Totem', and consider Lawrence's use of the primitive carvings as a controlling metaphor.

2. Ideas, Language

Women in Love V–VIII

You will already have noticed, from these early chapters of *Women in Love*, that the novel contains perhaps an unusual amount of intellectual discussion between characters. All novels employ dialogue to propose and explore the themes and ideas the author wants to develop: but usually the characters talk about their immediate concerns and experiences, while the author supplies, through some form of narrative or metaphorical context, a more philosophical background of theoretical ideas: this method, you may remember, is used in the opening conversation of *Women in Love*, the Brangwen sisters' discussion of marriage. The four central characters of the novel are, however, sophisticated and intellectually articulate people who can to a certain extent dispense with the mediation of the author and do their thinking for themselves. Examples from the first four chapters are the discussion of nationality in Chapter II (76–9); the conversation between Birkin and Gerald about spontaneity of behaviour (II.81–2); the argument between Birkin and Hermione in Chapter III (89–94); and the disagreements of Ursula and Gudrun in Chapter IV. Chapter V ('In the Train') consists mainly of a long discussion between Birkin and Gerald which gathers and defines most of the ideas already raised.

Read Chapter V now, and consider the following questions about this topic.

1   Look again at Birkin's arguments for 'spontaneity' of action in Chapter II, pp. 81–2, comparing them with Hermione's arguments in Chapter III (89–91), which Birkin attacks with such passionate vehemence. What's the relationship between their respective views?

2   Compare the following passages from Lawrence's own essay *Fantasia of the Unconscious* (1923) with the arguments exchanged in the novel. What light do these extracts throw on the debate between Birkin and Hermione in Chapter III?

> The first business of every faith is to declare its ignorance. I don't know where I came from – nor where I exit to. I don't know the origins of life nor the goal of death. I don't know how the two parent cells which are my biological origin became the me that I am.
>
> There should be no effort made to teach children to think, to have ideas. Only to lift them and urge them into dynamic activity. We can now see what is the true goal of education for a child . . . The aim is *not* mental consciousness. We want *effectual* human beings, not conscious ones. The final aim is not to *know, but to be* . . . Let all schools be closed at once.[1]

3   The character of Birkin is generally acknowledged to be, in some degree, a self-portrait of Lawrence himself.[2] Does this suggest that Birkin's arguments are likely to be charged with the weight

of the author's approval? Take into account this extract from a letter Lawrence wrote in December 1915 to Lady Ottoline Morrell, the real-life basis for the character of Hermione.[3]

Why are you so sad about your life? Only let go all this will to have things in your own control. We must all submit to be helpless and obliterated, quite obliterated, destroyed, cast away into nothingness. There is something will rise out of it, something new, that now is not. This which we are must cease to be, that we may come to pass in another being. Do not struggle with your will, to dominate your conscious life – do not do it. Only drift, and let go – let go, entirely, and become dark, quite dark – like winter which mows away all the leaves and flowers, and let only the dark underground roots remain. Let all the leaves and flowers and arborescent form of your life be cut off and cast away, all the old life, so that only the deep roots remain in the darkness underground, and you have no place in the light, no place at all. Let all knots be broken, all bonds unloosed, all connections slackened and released, all released, like the trees which release their leaves, and the plants which die away utterly above ground, let go all their being and pass away, only sleep in the profound darkness where being takes place again.

Do not keep your will in your *conscious* self. Forget, utterly forget, and let go. Let your will lapse back into your unconscious self, so you move in sleep, and in darkness, without sight or understanding. Only then will you act straight from the dark source of life outwards, which is creative life.

DISCUSSION

1   In Chapter II, you will remember, Birkin defended the unconventional behaviour of bride and groom at the Crich wedding by denying that 'standards', though necessary for the 'common ruck', need constrain the actions of people who matter: 'Anybody who is anything can just be himself and do as he likes' (II.81). 'It's the hardest thing in the world to act spontaneously on one's impulses . . . provided you're fit to do it' (II.82). In Chapter III we find Hermione putting a similar argument: 'do you think the children are better, richer, happier, for all this knowledge; do you really think they are? Or is it better to leave them untouched, spontaneous. Hadn't they better be animals, simple animals, crude, violent, anything, rather than this self-consciousness, this incapacity to be spontaneous' (III.90). Don't you feel there's a certain oddity in Birkin's violent rage against the assertion by another of his own ideas?

2   The oddity is compounded when we look at the extracts from Lawrence's essay *Fantasia of the Unconscious* and realize that the beliefs Hermione is stating are not only Birkin's, but were (or at least

were to become), the author's own. Hermione speaks for the same values – spontaneity, pre-conscious knowledge, the deathliness of the mind – that Lawrence affirms in his essay. Why should Lawrence create a self-portrait who then engages in a bitter attack against his creator's own ideas?

Let us look more closely at the grounds of Birkin's arguments. He asserts at first that consciousness is inevitable and knowledge desirable: 'Consciousness comes to them, willy-nilly'; 'Would you rather, for yourself, know or not know, that the little red flowers are there, putting out for the pollen?' (III.89). He then shifts his position, and attacks Hermione for being a slave to the very knowledge and mental consciousness she claims to reject: 'But knowing is everything to you, it is all your life' (III.89). Later he reverts to the first argument, contradicting what he has just said: young people are 'really dead', 'not because they have too much mind, but too little' (III.90). Subsequently he shifts again to the second: castigating Hermione's 'intellectualism', he blames her for valuing instinct, spontaneity and passion, only as ideas or mental concepts; like the Lady of Shallott, she watches the real world in a mirror. Her life is actually controlled not by the instincts and passions, but by her 'will':

> 'But your passion is a lie', he went on violently. 'It isn't passion at all, it is your *will*. It's your bullying will, you want to clutch things and have them in your power. And why? Because you haven't got any real body, any dark sensual body of life'.   (III.92)

Despite his earlier attempts to insist on the inevitability of consciousness, Birkin concludes by urging the destruction of the mind, the will and the self in a submission to some dark and indefinable power:

> '. . . sensuality . . . is a fulfilment – the great dark knowledge you can't have in your head – the dark involuntary being. It is death to oneself – but it is the coming into being of another . . . In the blood . . . when the mind and the known world is drowned in darkness – everything must go – there must be the deluge. Then you find yourself a palpable body of darkness, a demon.   (III.92–3).

3   Lawrence's letter to Lady Ottoline Morrell contains precisely the advice Birkin gives to Hermione and Ursula: though the private letter is written in the tone of concerned admonition, the fictional speech that of hostile invective. The terms of the argument, and the language in which it is expressed, clearly link the two passages together. In both appears the same opposition of values: 'will, control, power, volition, knowledge, intellect, understanding' are opposed to 'instinct, passion, spontaneity, sensuality'; 'knots, bonds and connections' are challenged by the concepts of 'release, sleep, lapsing back, drifting away, letting go'.

Clearly Birkin is very close to Lawrence himself here. The theory he articulates is identical to Lawrence's own philosophy; and furthermore the author, on the evidence of the letter, is evidently making use of an autobiographical situation. Here is an exposition, in a famous passage, of Lawrence's own belief in 'the blood':

> My great religion is a belief in the blood, the flesh, as being wiser than the intellect. We can go wrong in our minds. But what our blood feels and believes and says, is always true. The intellect is only a bit and a bridle. What do I care about knowledge. All I want is to answer to my blood, direct, without fribbling intervention of mind, or moral or what-not. I conceive a man's body as a kind of flame, forever upright and yet flowing: and the intellect is just the light that is shed on the things around. And I am not so much concerned with the things around – which is really mind – but with the mystery of the flame forever flowing . . .[4]

Consider this passage carefully: I will be referring back to it again. Is Lawrence arguing for a belief in pure instinct, a philosophy of irrationalism? What does the metaphor of the candle suggest about the relationship between body and mind, 'blood' and 'intellect'?

The evidence for a close identification of character and author is so strong that we must see Birkin as a spokesman for ideas Lawrence himself held. Does this also imply that the ideas argued for by the character are ideas the author wished to promote and affirm? Let us consider some of the different views that could be held about the status of intellectual ideas within the text, using this scene as an illustration. Below are three extracts from critical essays which bear on this problem. Consider each passage in turn, making notes on whatever implications you think it has for our interpretation of the debate between Birkin and Hermione.

(a) Hermione . . . is notoriously a portrait from life, sketched in one of Lawrence's extreme revulsions of feeling, after an initial admiration . . . Essentially, she is the type of possessive, intellectual-spiritual love, a love unwarmed by physical passion, desiring only to absorb and subjugate the mental being of its objects . . . Birkin treats her with consistent brutality . . . she rather feebly echoes his own eulogy of spontaneity and instinctual knowledge, . . . yet . . . her passion is purely mental, driven by the will, working through the understanding. (Graham Hough, 1956)[5]

(b) What Hermione utters . . . is what the world has been content to take for the pure Laurentian doctrine. Birkin repudiates it, with the violence of exasperation and disgust . . . But the dramatic projection remains wholly undisturbed, and what we have is more than a simple dissociation. Hermione, as Birkin himself (we recognize) could tell us, doesn't merely represent someone else's perversion of his 'doctrine'; the perversion is one he has had to take note of in his own inner experience. As he says of the school-children, 'consciousness comes to them, willy-nilly'; intelligence has its indispensable part . . . But mental consciousness brings with it the inevitable danger, and only a constant delicate concern for wholeness can ensure against the perversion that means a usurping domination from above. What Birkin denounces so brutally in Hermione is what he knows as a dangerous potentiality in himself.   (F. R. Leavis, 1955)[6]

(c)   The novel is a great discovery: far greater than Galileo's telescope or somebody else's wireless. The novel is the highest form of human expression so far attained. Why? Because it is so incapable of the absolute.

In a novel, everything is relative to everything else, if that novel is art at all. There may be didactic bits, but they aren't the novel. And the author may have didactic 'purpose' up his sleeve. Indeed most great novelists have, as Tolstoi had his Christian–socialism and Hardy his pessimism, and Flaubert his intellectual desparation. But even a didactic purpose so wicked as Tolstoi's or Flaubert's cannot put to death the novel.

You can tell me, Flaubert had a 'philosophy', not 'purpose'. But what is a novelist's philosophy but a purpose on a rather higher level? If only the 'purpose' be large enough, and not at odds with the passional inspiration.

. . . There you have the greatness of the novel itself. It won't *let* you tell didactic lies, and put them over.   (D. H. Lawrence, 1925)[7]

DISCUSSION

(a)   Graham Hough offers what probably seems the most straightforward explanation of the problem. This is to assume that there is no *intellectual* distinction between the views professed by Birkin and Hermione – both propound a philosophy which is essentially the author's own. We are intended therefore to regard the ideas themselves as valid and correct: but to see Hermione's attachment to them as only a 'feeble echo' of Birkin's faith, a species of intellectual hypocrisy by means of which she professes spontaneity but remains dominated by will and mental consciousness. Birkin's anger with her springs from her failure to live through the real consequences of her intellectual convictions. Hough further suggests that a similar disagreement sundered the mutual admiration of Lawrence and Ottoline Morrell.

Hough's reading has a certain objectivity absent from Leavis: he notes Birkin's 'brutality' without seeking to explain it as an implicit self-disgust. But he shows no awareness of any element of *contradiction* within the scene: Birkin's shifting line of argument, or the fact that he is denouncing the bullying of 'mental-consciousness' in an intensely bullying, highly mental and acutely conscious way.

(b)   Leavis' comments presuppose that there *is* a clear logical distinction between the arguments proposed: that Hermione's speeches are a distortion or fashionable vulgarization of Lawrence's 'doctrine': and that Birkin's rage against her is partly a prophet's sense of betrayal at an apostle's failure to profess the correct gospel, partly a violent reaction to his own predilection for 'mental consciousness'. What Lawrence was after, it is implied, was a clear distinction between the simplification and perversion of Lawrentian doctrine by Hermione, and Birkin's effort (by no means free from difficulty and temptation) to formulate the true gospel.

Leavis' account is characteristically subtle and persuasive. It allows for the fact that both lines of argument emanate from Lawrence's own theory of life. It insists, quite correctly, that Lawrence's own philosophy did not, like Hermione's, involve a negation of the intellect. Think back to the passage quoted earlier about Lawrence's 'great religion' (see above, p. 25). The metaphor of the candle defines intellect as the light cast on surrounding objects by the mysterious flame of physical being: one can't imagine a candle *without* light. The light, Lawrence insists, should be an emanation of the flesh and blood rather than a separate, artificial source of rational illumination from the 'mental-consciousness'. He is not so much devaluing the intellect as demanding a different and better adjustment of reason to the physical body.

On the other hand, there is a great deal in the passage that Leavis' account ignores. As we have found the arguments of both Birkin and Hermione exactly reduplicated in Lawrence's own opinions, is it quite so easy to distinguish the true gospel from its perversion? Doesn't Leavis also, like Hough, display an unwillingness to detect *contradiction* in the text? Isn't Birkin obviously using mental consciousness to argue against mental consciousness; exercising power in order to devalue power; straining by force of will to dislodge will from its pre-eminence – rather than displaying a 'constant delicate concern for wholeness'? If the product of Birkin's ethic is as Leavis proposes, a perfectly-adjusted moral being, why does Birkin himself imagine it as a 'demon' emerging from a deluge of darkness? (See below, pp. 48–56 for further discussion of the 'demonic' in *Women in Love*.)

(c)   Let us now consider Lawrence's own theoretical statement about the relation between fiction and ideas, and apply it to an evaluation of his own fictional practice. The main emphasis of his theoretical pronouncement is that ideas (or as he forcefully defines them, 'didactic lies') should always be subordinate to something larger and more important: which he defines here as the 'passional inspiration' that produces great novels. Good fiction springs from deeper sources of being than the intellect or reason. When a novelist has an over-riding didactic idea, purpose or philosophy, it can work to destroy the novel, unless the 'passional inspiration' from the author's whole being can subdue it to its proper role. Lawrence further argues that the 'relative' nature of the novel form co-operates with the 'passional inspiration' to keep intellect under control – the novel is 'incapable of the absolute', in a novel 'everything is relative to everything else'. Any didactic assertion, abstract idea or philosophical theory advanced in a novel will inevitably be qualified, modified, perhaps even subverted by the contingent presence of other ideas, psychological factors, circumstantial details.

Doesn't this provide us with a different way of reading the debate between Birkin and Hermione? Consider some of the factors we discussed in Chapter One: dramatic situation, methods of characterization, and narrative technique. The 'class-room' situation, you remember, could be used to reflect ironically on Birkin's passionate determination to persuade: 'Both women were hostile and resentful. He sounded as if he were addressing a meeting' (III.94). Later in the novel, Ursula frequently criticizes Birkin's tendency to appear as 'a Sunday-school teacher, a prig of the stiffest type' (XI.190). The fact that Birkin doesn't succeed in convincing or persuading anybody is surely also a reflection on his powers as a prophet and teacher. Consider also the *way* in which Hermione's arguments are proferred, the acutely affected manner of tortured intensity which so irritates Birkin, and perhaps tells us more about her than the ideas themselves do: 'her face puckered, her brow was knit with thought, she seemed twisted in troublesome effort for utterance' (III.89); 'she wiped her fingers across her brow, with a vague weariness' (III.90). Those narratorial details surely establish a contradiction between the gospel of spontaneity Hermione is articulating, and the actual psychological condition she speaks from. Birkin too, as we have observed, is a focus of contradictions, the subject of a self-division which perhaps accounts for the lack of consistency, the presence of contradiction in his arguments. This being the case, Birkin is not going to function effectively or straightforwardly as a vehicle for the persuasive communication of the author's ideas.

Lawrence's theory of the novel implies a whole complex of fictional elements (characters, stories, descriptions, etc.) in which the exchange of ideas performs a particular function in a larger design. The ideas themselves, whatever their provenance and authority, are made 'relative to everything else': so that we are not confronted directly with the responsibility for accepting or denying them. We are presented rather with a dramatic conflict in which the exchange of ideas forms part of a complex and contradictory human totality.

This question should certainly be left open, however, and we will be returning to it. It remains to be proved, with regard to the novel as a whole, that Lawrence did in fact succeed in implementing his theory of fiction as the production of a relative totality of experience in which the novelist's didactic purpose is subdued to his 'passional inspiration'. You may feel, when all is said, that as Birkin is the only person who *does* effectively articulate a philosophy, which no one else successfully challenges (except by rejection) his ideas remain standing simply by default. We will consider the whole matter again in later chapters (see below, pp. 82–96); and now in relation to Chapter V.

Read Chapter V of *Women in Love*, ('In the Train'), and consider the following questions:

1   How do you react to Birkin's assertions about the decadence of his society, the hypocrisy of class-consciousness, the emptiness of material prosperity, the possibility of 'ultimate marriage' as a 'single pure activity' which will bring meaning to an utterly sterile and purposeless existence? (V.105–110). Does the narrative seem to validate or endorse his ideas?

2   Does the presence of Gerald as an interlocutor modify our responses to Birkin's arguments? In other words, is the didacticism of Birkin's position controlled by the dramatic situation?

3   Look carefully at Birkin's apocalyptic meditation on p. 111: 'Well, if mankind is destroyed . . . ' What do you think of his ideas? Do you think the novel requires us to take them seriously?

Below I have assembled some passages which will help you in your explanation of these questions. They are not clues to the correct answer, but raw material for the production of your own interpretation.

(a)   . . . over the river, beyond the ferry, there is the flat silvery world, as in the beginning, untouched . . . and no people, no people at all . . . It is a great thing to realize that the original world is still there – perfectly clean and pure . . . It is the mass of unclean world that we have superimposed on the clean world that we cannot bear. (D. H. Lawrence, 1915)[10]

I think truly the only righteousness is the destruction of mankind, as in Sodom . . . if one could but have a great box of insect powder, and shake it over them, in the heavens, and exterminate them. Only to cleanse and purify the beautiful earth, and give room for some truth and pure living.   (D. H. Lawrence, 1916)[9]

(b)   Lawrence, the whole creative artist, enacts a tentative or kind of experimental process – a testing and exploring of the conscious and formulated conclusions that Birkin thinks he has settled in securely enough to act upon. *Has* he? What in the concrete do they really amount to? Do they involve any self-deception or illusion or unreality? Those questions the thoroughly dramatic Birkin enacts. Self-dramatized in Birkin, the Lawrence who formulates conclusions ('doctrines') and ponders them suffers exposure to the searching tests and the impersonal criteria that the artist's creative genius, which represents an impersonal profundity and wholeness of being, implicitly and impartially applies to them. The creative work itself is not to be taken as offering any such conclusions except in so far as the reader feels that the 'tale' does in fact endorse, concretely define, and convey them.   (F. R. Leavis, 1955)[10]

(c)   Birkin . . . does not go entirely uncriticized: but it is significant that what qualifying judgements surround him concern not so much what he says, as the didactic manner in which he says it. If his position is not to be taken as wholly Lawrentian, it is not an account of other viewpoints in the novel which might challenge it: no such alternatives are available. So we are forced to conclude that Birkin's remarks merit serious attention, despite their flavour of contemptuous, neurotic externality posturing as reflective wisdom:

'We have an ideal of a perfect world, clean and straight and sufficient. So we cover the earth with foulness; life is a blotch of labour, like insects scurrying in filth, so that your collier can have a pianoforte in his parlour, and you can have a butler and a motor-car in your up-to-date house, and as a nation we can sport the Ritz or the Empire, Gaby Deslys and the Sunday newspapers. It is very dreary.'

. . . the generalized superficiality suggested by this lame collection of cant phrases is now much more a quality of the observer's standpoint than of what is observed. The world, in Birkin's own terms, is 'extraneous' to creative individuality; and from this detached, disgusted viewpoint, society can be abstracted to a petty, ephemeral exhalation of a non-human creative urge. (Terry Eagleton, 1970)[11]

DISCUSSION

1   This is partly, of course, a matter of opinion. I should imagine that most readers would feel that there is much of value in what Birkin has to say; but that the extreme position he adopts, and the

imprecision of the language he employs make it difficult for the reader to endorse and accept his intellectual perspective. Many of Birkin's views are the common currency of twentieth-century 'liberal' thought, so few people would find it difficult to assent to at least some of them: the view that modern industrial society tends to neglect deeper human purposes; the idea that material prosperity doesn't guarantee meaningful existence; the proposition that class-consciousness and status symbols don't of themselves bring human fulfilment; the affirmation that love can be a means of realizing meaning in an otherwise sterile and meaningless world. But who can follow Birkin to the extremity of his chiliastic vision: to his belief that the human world as we know it is merely an alien superimposition on the pristine innocence of nature; and that the only prospect for a thorough cleansing of that world, a restoration of its original nature, would be its total annihilation? Furthermore, Birkin's ideas are again contradictory: '. . . This beautiful evening with the luminous land and trees . . .' (V.111) is essentially a *human evaluation* of what is seen: with mankind destroyed, there would be no agent capable of attributing 'beauty' to the landscape the man is perceiving. Convinced of the universality of corruption and decadence, the individual withdraws into an isolation so acute that he can feel relationship only with a vaguely-realized force of evolution, a 'creative mystery'. This presents the reader with a problem greater than the difficulty of assessing a character with eccentric views: for in pronouncing humanity a 'dead letter', Birkin is breaking all contract of sympathy between character and reader. This amounts almost to a personal betrayal for each reader: *you* too are being told that you are a dead letter, and should arrange to pass away as quickly and conveniently as possible.

2   The device of embodying Birkin's statements and propositions in a dialogue with Gerald is more than a mere narrative convenience. As in the discussion between Birkin and the two women in Chapter III, we can measure the effectiveness of Birkin's ideas against the reactions he provokes in his interlocutors. In the conversation with Gerald, for example, it is abundantly clear that Gerald is not persuaded by Birkin's arguments, that he remains aloof and detached: curious and interested, but finally unconvinced. Naturally there are different ways of reading this distinction between the two men. If Birkin's ideas are proven in the course of the novel to be correct, then Gerald's unwillingness to take him seriously (see V.110) will inevitably stand as a charge against Gerald. On the other hand, if the exchange of ideas operates in a truly *dramatic* manner, as a clash of ideas directed towards the neutral perspective of an objective

curiosity, then both Birkin and his statements are, as Leavis would say, 'placed': located into a dramatic context which relativizes, qualifies and criticizes any didactic intention. It is true, as Terry Eagleton argues, that Birkin's point-of-view is the only one that gets effectively articulated: Gerald's inquisitions and reticences may suggest some effort to qualify Birkin's utterances, but they scarcely amount to a point-of-view which could challenge Birkin's assertions. But Gerald may perhaps be designed to function as a sceptical surrogate reader: there to react for us, to encourage us to deflect the didactic thrust of the character's driving moral 'purpose'. Gerald seems able to detect where Birkin's utterances are assertive rather than authoritative: 'But to Gerald it sounded as if he were insistent rather than confident' (V.109); and Birkin's observations of the other man seem to involve an admiring tribute to Gerald's courage in the face of tragedy, an acknowledgement that Gerald's way may be desperately pessimistic, yet possess the validity of a certain stoic heroism: 'Birkin could not help seeing how beautiful and soldierly his face was, with a certain courage to be indifferent'. The chapter ends with the two men confronting London in diametrically opposite ways: Birkin with his melodramatic despair, Gerald with an excitement of anticipation:

> And Birkin who, for some reason was now tired and dispirited, said to him:
> 'I always feel doomed when the train is running into London. I feel such a despair, so hopeless, as if it were the end of the world'.
> 'Really!' said Gerald. 'And does the end of the world frighten you?'
> Birkin lifted his shoulders in a slow shrug.
> 'I don't know.' he said. 'It does while it hangs imminent and doesn't fall. But people give me a bad feeling – very bad.'
> There was a roused glad smile in Gerald's eyes.
> 'Do they?' he said. And he watched the other man critically.
> (V.113)

Gerald could here be voicing and displaying, on behalf of the reader, a critical scepticism towards Birkin's apocalyptic misanthropy. Or perhaps he is actually roused to excitement at the prospect of an 'end of the world', a final adventure; in which case the novel proposes to the reader a genuine alternative, in the choice between Gerald's heroic resignation and Birkin's weary despair.

Let us now consider again the possibility of an authorial intervention into the narrative through Birkin's statements and meditations. The passages from Lawrence's letters indicate that Birkin is voicing some of the author's own feelings and convictions in the period when the novel was written. (Lawrence's personal experiences of this period need to be considered in their context of Britain in the First World War: they are discussed below, Chapter Six.)

Possibly Birkin is the author's mouthpiece, employed to persuade the reader of certain propositions. F. R. Leavis however (above, p. 30) argues that the presentation of Birkin is wholly impersonal and dramatic, so that the novelist cannot be accused of pressing his own didactic purposes on the reader. Leavis admits that there is a tendency in Birkin towards didacticism, a penchant for formulating oversimplified solutions to complex problems; and that this tendency reflects a trait in Lawrence himself. But in the context of the novel, Leavis insists, this didactic trait is fully controlled and integrated into a balanced totality: Birkin's formulated opinions are presented as the views of a character, not the settled conclusions of the author. By this means, Lawrence protected himself from the dangers of his own didactic impulses: Leavis frequently quotes Lawrence's aphorism, 'never trust the artist – trust the tale'; the writer himself may be opinionated and didactic, but the work itself – provided it successfully embodies the author's 'passional inspiration' – will control those polemical impulses and subdue them to a larger, integrated design. Leavis' arguments here of course base themselves in Lawrence's own theory of fiction.

3   Terry Eagleton describes Birkin's vision of the end of the world as a 'petty, ephemeral exhalation' of the character's 'detached, disgusted viewpoint': that it is a desperate bid for significance on the part of an imagination atrophied by misanthropy. If you felt sympathetic to Eagleton's views, you would probably regard Birkin's faith in the power of an 'incomprehensible' creative force to evolve an alternative to humanity, as a vision lacking either the intellectual conviction of science, the doctrinal consistency of religion, or the imaginative power of myth: the force itself is given so little substance that it neither convinces the reason, sways the faith, nor compels the imagination.

The problem of the exact status and validity of ideas in the text can thus be resolved into a basic question: is the novel dogmatic, designed to force the author's ideas onto the reader by valorizing the character who speaks them, or demonstrating that certain ideas are correct and others false? Or does it answer rather to Lawrence's own stipulations, and succeed in subduing ideas to a larger design in which they have an important though subordinate place? We have seen that Birkin is not allowed to act simply as a spokesman, that the expression of his ideas is criticized and deflected by the reactions of other characters. But do Birkin's views remain standing simply by default, since no one else in the novel formulates an effective philosophy to compete with his?

You might look forward in the novel to some other passages

where ideas figure importantly in the design of the narrative: Chapter XIII ('Mino'), pp. 206–216, Chapter XIX ('Moony'), pp. 325–32, Chapter XXIX ('Continental'), pp. 523–9. All these passages are discussed below, in Chapter Three, pp. 58–60; Chapter Five, pp. 84–9; and Chapter Six, pp. 71–4.

It is an axiom of traditional literary criticism that the difference between ideas as they appear in a philosophical treatise, and as they are embodied in a work of literature, consists in the greater complexity and richer capacity for meaning conferred on them by literary form and language. Whether or not we agree with that view, it is obviously important to consider the special and unique features of language which distinguish literary discourse from other kinds of writing.

I would like you to move forward in the text of *Women in Love* to Chapter VIII ('Breadalby'), where we will find some useful illustrations of Lawrence's use of language. Read now the whole of that chapter, which shows Birkin deciding he has 'had enough' of the whole Breadalby scene, and culminates in Hermione's violent assault on him. Once again, the emotional conflict between them is partly fought out by means of a clash of ideas (see especially VIII.140–2 and 161).

But for this exercise on language I would like you to focus particularly on two passages: (1) pp. 162–3, 'He went into the boudoir' to 'fulfilment of this perfect ecstasy'; (2) pp. 165–7, from 'Yet he wanted something' to 'happy and unquestioned, by himself'. Consider Lawrence's use of language in these passages, and make some notes on the following questions:

1   Passage (1) could be summarized: 'Hermione found Birkin's presence an intolerable obstruction, and desired intensely to be free of it'. What would be lost in such a précis?
2   Does the use of language seem to you successful in communicating meaning and emotion?
3   Would you say the device of repeating words and phrases was overdone, or justified by the effects Lawrence achieves?

Use the critical extracts printed below to help you in formulating some conclusions on this matter.

(a)   In point of style, fault is often found with the continued, slightly modified repetition. The only answer is that it is natural to the author; and that every natural crisis in emotion or passion or understanding comes from this pulsing, frictional to-and-fro which works up to culmination.   (D. H. Lawrence, 1920)[12]

(b) . . . after forming a higher opinion of *Women in Love* at each re-reading in the course of nearly thirty years, I still do not question that the book *has* faults. The most obvious and the worst . . . is that in . . . places Lawrence betrays by an insistent and over-emphatic explicitness, running at times to something one can only call jargon, that he is uncertain – uncertain of the value of what he offers; uncertain whether he really holds it – whether a valid communication has really been defined and conveyed in terms of creative art.   (F. R. Leavis, 1955)[13]

(c) Lawrence himself realized there was something unusual about the language of *Women in Love*. It was his declared intention to go 'a stratum deeper than I think anybody has ever gone, in a novel' . . . He wished, in other words, to work at a level deeper than that of everyday consciousness, and quickly came to the conclusion that the 'hard, violent style, full of sensation and presentation', in which he had written *Sons and Lovers*, was not adaptable for this purpose . . . there seems to me still a persistent lack of fit between the actual world and the portrait of it in *Women in Love*; a lack of fit caused by Lawrence's deliberate withdrawal from 'sensation and presentation'.

    We can only conclude that Lawrence, in 1913, found himself in the position of Aesop's dog, and dropped the bone of concrete presentation, while pursuing the glimmering image of 'deeper strata' and 'allotropic states'. Yet, if language is anything to go by, these states were as difficult to grasp as the reflected bone; and one may well suspect that they had no more reality . . . Certainly a sense of the author straining over and over again to capture the uncapturable pervades *Women in Love*. It is precisely this straining which produces the inflation and repetition we have noted . . .   (Derek Bickerton, 1967)[14]

(d) If we are irritated by this prose I suggest the most likely reason is that we are reading it the wrong way and refusing to allow the tone to carry us. If we read with the alertness and expectations proper to a *Times* leader we shall certainly often object 'he's said that before'. But Lawrence is not here conducting an argument in which restatement is unnecessary repetition . . . new contexts . . . make the same phrase express a further emotional develop-ment, not by describing or naming the emotion but by imagina-tively creating it. Every phrase is relative to every other phrase, and the passage is a whole, though the relations and the unity are not those we expect of ordinary prose . . . We have a direct sympathy with these movements of feeling because the lan-guage has the air of following the experience, the 'pulsing, frictional to-and-fro' as it arises in the consciousness of the characters . . . This prose is, in a word, poetic, enacting an experience with a depth we do not expect from ordinary prose. (Ian Robinson, 1978)[15]

DISCUSSION

The most obvious stylistic feature of both passages is of course *repetition*: the repeating of words, phrases, images and ideas. In passage (1) the words chaos, darkness, struggle, break, wall, presence, obstruction, electricity, voluptuous, consummation, strong, delight, ecstasy, are all employed more than once. An idea that could be articulated in the form of a simple statement is here expressed by means of two separable series of phrases, which run in parallel and flow into one another, though each continuously expresses a single idea. The basic assertion, made with reference to Hermione's consciousness, that Birkin is an 'obstruction' or metaphorically a 'wall', is repeated in no fewer than eight separable phrases:

- like being walled up
- his presence was the wall
- his presence was obstructing her
- walled up in horror
- he was the wall
- the awful obstruction
- him who obstructed her life
- an unthinkable evil obstruction

At the same time, as a kind of counter-movement to the rhetoric of 'obstruction', a parallel series of phrases expresses Hermione's resistance:

- unless she could break out
- she must break down the wall
- she must break him down
- it must be done

In the following paragraphs (VIII.163) the two parallel sequences are initiated by 'voluptuous thrill' and 'voluptuous consummation'. Again, a bald summary of the passage could encapsulate the basic meaning in a few words: 'Hermione felt sufficiently strong to satisfy her desire to destroy Birkin'. But Lawrence's prose elaborates that simple idea into a rhythmic dialectic of desire and fulfilment:

– terrible voluptuous thrill	– voluptuous consummation
– what delight	– consummation of voluptuous ecstasy
– delirium of pleasure	– perfect unutterable consummation
– voluptuous ecstasy	– unutterable satisfaction
– extremity of bliss	– her ecstasy was consummated
– unconscious in ecstasy	– the fulfilment of this perfect ecstasy
– convulsion of pure bliss	

Four sub-motifs are interwoven into the two central currents of meaning (1) the notion of strength – 'her arms were strong', 'irrestibly strong', 'what delight in strength'; (2) the metaphor of electricity, used to describe some powerful emotional force which she releases, yet which blasts her: 'shocks of electricity', 'volts of electricity', 'fluid lightning'; (3) the suggestion that Hermione's emotions are – or seem to her – 'pure': 'a pure flame', 'purely unconscious in ecstasy'; and (4) the references to the ball of lapis lazuli with which she strikes Birkin: 'a blue, beautiful ball', 'she rolled it round in her hand', 'the ball of jewel stone'.

It would surely be an inadequate response to this complex prose to argue that Lawrence is making something essentially simple into something unnecessarily elaborate and difficult. We wouldn't be very interested in fiction that worked by paring away all unnecessary detail to arrive at some lowest common denominator of language. Even prose-writers who have sought to attain a maximum of directness, clarity and simplicity – such as Ernest Hemingway – have still relied on rhythmic effects, verbal and phrasal repetition, the elaboration of language to achieve various 'poetic' effects. Furthermore, the language of simple direct statement perhaps belongs to the 'old-fashioned human element', the 'certain moral scheme' Lawrence explicitly rejected: perhaps his avowed preoccupation with 'deeper being' entailed the development of a complex prose style. Nevertheless, isn't there perhaps a case for arguing that Lawrence is overdoing the technique here, substituting rhetorical repetition and hypnotic rhythms for a clear, direct, concrete statement of what he means?

Evidently many critics, as you can see from the passages quoted, are of that opinion. Earlier we saw John Middleton Murray complaining that the writing is 'inaccessible' and apparently directionless: its rhythms are the unintelligible 'beating' of an underground sea (see above, Chapter I, p. 2). F. R. Leavis (who was not thinking particularly of this passage from the novel) suggested that the 'insistent and over-emphatic' style betrays not only a lack of clarity, but a deep uncertainty on the part of the author about 'the value' of what he offers. Does Lawrence employ repetition as a form of rhetorical insistence? Derek Bickerton argues emphatically that this is so: Lawrence was attempting to 'capture the uncapturable', to describe something he believed to be there, beyond the real world, but which proves on the evidence of the language, to be an unreality. Does the writing display qualities of 'inflation' and 'repetition' because it is 'straining' beyond the parameters of objective reality, seeking to describe some elusive, probably non-existent supra-reality?

Let us consider the critical extracts that defend the novel's technique. Lawrence's self-defence begins with a polemical gesture: repetition is 'natural to the author'. This is surely no defence at all, since what is natural to the author may be bad writing. His second point is more illuminating: 'every natural crisis in emotion or passion or understanding comes from this pulsing, frictional to-and-fro which works up to culmination'. Using language which sounds more like a description of the sexual act than a comment on the rhythm of prose, Lawrence argues that the style is designed to *imitate* or *represent* the rhythm and movement of experience – 'emotion or passion or understanding'. If we applied this account to the passage we have been considering from Chapter VIII, we would find Lawrence's theory confirmed. There are in the prose examples of that 'to-and-fro' rhythm: between Hermione's awareness of 'darkness' and 'chaos', and her 'struggle' against them; between her sense of being 'walled up' and her desire to 'break out'; between the voluptuous pleasure she feels in contemplating violence, and the desire to satisfy it in destruction. The dialectical rhythm 'pulses' to a consummation as she smashes the stone onto Birkin's head. The prose is less a technique of statement than a mode of presenting feelings. Robinson follows Lawrence's assertions and argues that the technique of phrasal repetition works 'not by describing or naming the emotion but by imaginatively creating it'. Once the prose has 'realized the feelings' it has the capacity to draw the reader into sympathy with the characters: 'We have a direct sympathy with these movements of feeling because the language has the air of following the experience, the "pulsing, frictional to-and-fro" as it arises in the consciousness of the characters'.

Here then is one way of validating Lawrence's prose technique: by appealing to the author's own theory of 'being', accepting his emphasis on unconscious physical and emotional forces, and declaring the prose to be a mimetic form for representing the deepest rhythms of experience.

Let us bear in mind also some of the problems raised by this solution. If Lawrence's prose can successfully involve the reader in an immediate engagement with an embodied experience, then two things follow: (1) the technique should work equally well for *any* kind of experience, making the destructive lust of a would-be murderer as imaginatively compelling as the struggles of the murderer's victim; and (2) the reader is likely to lose, as he/she is drawn through current after current of unconscious experience, any sense of intellectual control or moral orientation.

1 Compare the use of language in the passage discussed above with that of *Women in Love*, Chapter VIII, pp.165–6. Is Lawrence using similar techniques? With a similar, or very different effect?
2 Do you find yourself more sympathetically involved in Birkin's experience than in Hermione's?

DISCUSSION

The prose techniques are very similar, are they not? Again the principle device is that of repetition of words, phrases, images and ideas. Again there are two parallel but conflicting currents of feeling, which can be separated thus:

- He wanted to touch them
- saturate himself with the touch
- moving his feet softly
- letting them touch his belly
- such a fine, cool, subtle touch
- saturate himself with their contact
- soft as a breath, soft
- delicate and more beautiful
- coolness and subtlety of vegetation
- lovely, subtle, responsive vegetation
- perfect cool loneliness
- lovely and fresh
- lovely and cool and desirable
- lovely, subtle, responsive vegetation

The one series emphasizes softness and delicacy of touch, coolness and subtlety of contact, and with words like 'saturate' suggests the merging of the human being into a perfect union with the vegetation. The other series emphasizes contradictory sensations, hardness and sharpness:

- sharp boughs beat upon him
- beat his loins
- sharp needles
- a thistle which pricked him
- to sting one's thigh
- dark bristles
- light whip of the hazel
- stinging
- hardness

A third series emphasizes ideas of happiness, arrival, belonging:

 – He was happy
 – how fulfilled he was, how happy
 – enriched immeasurably
 – one knew where one belonged
 – he knew now where he belonged
 – to plant himself, his seed
 – this was his place, his marriage place

A further contradiction is introduced into this sequence as Birkin thinks of the world he is abandoning: he contrasts the 'new state' to the 'old ethic', prefers his 'madness' to 'the regular sanity'. Again the repetitions formulate a rhythm designed to induce emotional acquiescence in the reader: the 'pulsing, frictional to-and-fro' enacts Birkin's experience with a vivid concreteness that draws us into imaginative sympathy.

Do we sympathize more with Birkin's experience than with Hermione's? You may well feel that we *ought* to sympathize more closely with the victim than the would-be murderer. You may also feel that the poetry of Birkin's experience (the softness of touch, the beauty of living things, the survival of creativity) is obviously preferable to the poetry of Hermione's (a poetry of violence, resistance, the pleasure of destruction). Yet the choice is not really so easy. The intensity of Birkin's disillusionment with humanity isolates him into a condition of complete estrangement, where it is surely difficult for the reader to follow. It is one thing to talk of loving nature: but what Birkin experiences is a kind of sexual communion with grass and trees and flowers: 'He knew where to plant himself, his seed; – along with the trees, in the folds of delicious fresh-growing leaves' (VIII.166). This intense union with nature is explicitly defined as a recoil from humanity: 'What a dread he had of mankind, of other people!' (VIII.166). The explicitness of the sexual metaphors makes Birkin's state of mind harder to sympathize with: since we know that human beings cannot survive, even at the biological level, in isolation; you can't marry grass and trees, or reproduce by making love to a leaf. The implications of this estrangement are not shirked or ignored: Birkin himself declares his state to be one of 'madness': though it is preferable to 'the regular sanity'.

Hermione's lust to destroy is as rhythmically evocative of an emotional experience as Birkin's effort of recovery – and as capable of entrancing the reader into empathetic association. Are we supposed to make any moral distinction between them? Is the blood-lust of the murderer as valid as the self-defensive survival of the victim?

The questions confront us much more sharply with the potential problems involved in Lawrence's revolutionary concept of 'being', and in his radically experimental fictional techniques: it is apparent from certain clear suggestions that Lawrence is saying exactly that. 'It was quite right of Hermione to want to kill him', says Birkin (167). Earlier, in Chapter I, Birkin had sought to persuade Gerald that in every murder there is a murderer and a murderee: that the victim has a will to be destroyed corresponding to the murderer's destructive lust. If Birkin's philosophy is to be credited, there can be no real harm in Hermione trying to kill him: he will die only if he wishes to be murdered. Perhaps Hermione's destructive passion is as valid and defensible a response to the given situation as Birkin's determination to survive by isolation, alienation and madness. Perhaps the reader isn't being offered a moral dilemma, but only a choice of experiences.

A further footnote to this discussion concerns the validity of these 'mimetic' premises proposed by Lawrence, followed by F. R. Leavis, and followed in turn by Ian Robinson. Obviously Lawrence's theory of imitation is entirely different from the nineteenth-century concept of 'realism' – the confidence in literature's power to represent objective reality accurately and truthfully. Yet it still remains a belief in the capacity of fiction to represent (enact, dramatize, present) *something* – deeper being, transcendent reality, 'life'. The traditional view that literature is imitative of an objective reality has been seriously eroded by radical changes in the intellectual climate of European and American literary criticism, originally as a result of the influence of French structuralism. Modern 'post-structuralist' literary criticism questions whether language really *does* imitate an external reality: and proposes instead that all 'reality' is in fact constructed in language. Thus we have to consider whether Lawrence's attempt to represent a truer or deeper reality of human experience is anything more than a refinement of nineteenth-century realism: a new mimesis in which, though the object of imitation has changed, the method has only shifted its focus.

* * *

We are now in a position to recognize the validity of those early bewildered readers' reactions with which we began in Chapter One. Lawrence's fictional techniques evidently were so radically experimental and avant-garde that instantaneous comprehension of his novel could hardly be imagined. Those critics who argued that the characters could not be distinguished were in a sense correct: for Lawrence himself asserted that all expressions of character are really

manifestations of a single, radically-unchanged element. So if there
are important distinctions between people to be made, they need to
be made at a level below egoistic 'personality' or socially-observable
behaviour. Those readers who considered the characters abnormal
and peculiar were also, surely, responding to real characteristics of
the novel: a character like Birkin almost defines himself in terms of
his abnormality. The accusation that the novel is static was a
symptomatic response to Lawrence's departure from the familiar
norms of nineteenth-century 'plot' and 'narrative'; and the criticisms
of the style an acknowledgement that Lawrence's prose was seeking
unprecedented fictional effects. It will be as well to remember the
spontaneous reistance of those contemporary readers, as we proceed
in the next chapter to examine the writing of the critic who, in the
1950s, fiercely opposed all received opinions about Lawrence,
demanded a complete revision of approaches to his writing, and
utterly transformed the way in which people read and thought about
his fiction: F. R. Leavis.

What, meanwhile, have we learned about 'ideas' and 'language'
in *Women in Love*? Pre-eminently, I think, the fact that they are actually interdependent and closely inter-related: though I have separated one from the other for convenience of discussion, it will
become increasingly evident to you that 'ideas' are often expressed
'poetically' and metaphorical language is used to express ideas. Intellectual controversies tend to collapse, as we have seen, into
psychological dramas; and there is always a rich, suggestive, complex flow of impressions (details of character, narrative hints, physical descriptions, images and symbols) to modify, comment on or
even subvert any bare intellectual statement. In the brilliant chapter
of *Women in Love* entitled 'Mino' (Chapter XIII, discussed
in my Chapter Three) a debate about love, conducted in terms
of argument between characters, is resolved (in one way or another)
by the intervention of a scene between two cats, who enact a fable
which serves as a symbolic reflection on human motives and purposes. I will be discussing similar uses of symbolic or metaphorical
scenes below: Chapter XIX ('Moony') is handled at Chapter Five,
pp. 84–9; and Chapter XVIII ('Rabbit') at Chapter Four, pp. 65–8.
You might test what you have learned about language on a difficult
passage from later in the novel: Chapter XXIII 'Excurse', especially pages 394–403, discussed below, Chapter Five, 96–101. Or
you could look ahead to Chapter XIV ('Water-Party') for examples
of the fusion of language and ideas (discussed below, Chapter Three,
pp. 49–54).

3. Creativity, Dissolution

Women in Love IX–XIV

By examining the novel's methods of narrative and characterization, its use of language and its presentation of ideas, we have considered the most important *formal* problems involved in reading it. Your own reading can now be accompanied by a constant attentiveness to these artistic devices. I will now move on to a consideration of the overall design and structure of *Women in Love*. As we have seen, Lawrence did not employ traditional nineteenth-century fictional techniques in his handling of plot, character and language: but the novel's most obvious structural device – a sustained comparison and contrast between two love-relationships and their respective social contexts – Lawrence inherited from an acknowledged masterpiece of classic nineteenth-century realism, Tolstoi's *Anna Karenina*. The avant-garde techniques of *Women in Love* seem to have obscured this feature for many early readers (see above, Chapter One, pp. 2–3) who complained that the contrast or distinction wasn't clear enough. It is probably no accident that the first really influential and persuasive critical account of Lawrence's work was particularly concerned to stress the novelist's relationship with 'tradition', and to clarify the distinction between the two relationships in *Women in Love* to a point where they could no longer conceivably be confused. I refer to the critic F. R. Leavis, who was also responsible for establishing the centrality of *Women in Love* within the canon of Lawrence's works. One of Leavis' earliest publications was a pamphlet, *D. H. Lawrence* (1930); he transformed the whole character of Lawrence criticism through a series of essays published in the academic journal *Scrutiny*, eventually compiled into the book *D. H. Lawrence: Novelist* (1955); and one of his last publications was a second full-length book, *Thought, Words and Creativity: Art and Thought in Lawrence* (1976).[1]

Leavis evaluated *Women in Love* as 'one of the most striking works of creative originality fiction has to show'.[2] He saw the novel as a masterpiece of 'art' and a great achievement of 'thought' (the two key, related terms that dominate all his writing on Lawrence), which can provide readers of the present with a most necessary diagnostic analysis of the deep malaise of twentieth-century industrial civilization. This searching analysis of modern industrial society is naturally focused on the mine-owner Gerald Crich: 'In Gerald we see the malady of the individual as the essential process of industrial civilization'[3]. What Gerald represents, in both his private identity and his public role, is the domination of will and 'mental-consciousness' over the 'spontaneous-creative' life of the passions and instincts. In himself Gerald sustains a deep psychic damage from this violation of the physical and instinctual being: his personal relationships fail, and his life ends in a sterile and meaningless death, a 'barren tragedy' (XXXI.577). As a progressive capitalist bent on producing a perfect industrial order in which both matter and human beings are thoroughly subordinated to the control of will, Gerald succeeds in developing a mechanized society, empty of purpose and meaning, to mirror the hollowness of his own starved psyche.

Over against this portrayal of the malady, according to Leavis' account, Lawrence offered his readers an illustration of a corrective norm, in the relationship of Birkin and Ursula. Where the mode of existence represented by Gerald leads to disaster, and the relationship he has with Gudrun – in itself 'mechanized' and self-destructive – breaks down, the marriage of Birkin and Ursula is held to constitute a positive alternative:

> A strong normative preoccupation, entailing positives that are concretely present in many ways (we have them above in the phrases, 'the goodness, the holiness, the desire for creation and productive happiness') informs the life of *Women in Love* . . . In Birkin's married relations with Ursula the book invites us to localize the positive, the conceivable and due – if only with difficulty attainable – solution of the problem; the norm, in relation to which Gerald's disaster gets its full meaning . . .[4]

As you can see from the above quotations, Leavis' conception of the novel evokes a simple structure based on a pattern of moral antitheses. The psychological equilibrium of Birkin is contrasted with the emotional disorder of Gerald; the positive creativity of the

Birkin–Ursula relationship is opposed to the tragic self-destructiveness of Gudrun and Gerald's. The structure remains intact despite the large number of qualifications and reservations with which Leavis hedges it about. Though he refers constantly to difficulties, complexities, local weaknesses, his fundamental argument rests on the premise of an effective moral distinction between a growing and a doomed relationship.

Please give a careful reading to *Women in Love* Chapter IX, pp. 168–72 (from the beginning to 'soft blood-subordination, terrible'). Then examine Leavis' comments on the passage, and consider the questions that follow.

> To suggest the range and flexibility of Lawrence's art one may set over against 'The Industrial Magnate' the earlier chapter (IX), 'Coal-dust', in which Gerald forces his terror-stricken Arab mare to stand while the colliery train passing the level crossing does its worst with wheels, brakes, buffers, chains and whistle. The whole thing is rendered with shattering immediacy; with Ursula and Gudrun we stand, tortured by hideous noise and clenched in violent protest, while the rider compels the frantic mare back against herself and into the assaulting terrors . . . We now realize the energy of will in Gerald as something more cruelly and dangerously ruthless than, for instance, it appears as Ursula and Gudrun discuss it in Chapter IV, 'Diver'.[5]

1 In his commentary, Leavis argues that the scene is dramatized from the sisters' point-of-view, with which the reader identifies. Is that correct? Are the sisters as united in feeling as Leavis suggests? Is no other narrative perspective introduced? Has the reader no choice but to identify with an emotion of 'violent protest'?

2 Leavis observes that there is no authorial comment to orientate the reader's attitude towards the experience: nonetheless, he feels that the poetic and dramatic art carries with it an inescapable moral imperative. Is it the case that only one view of the episode is possible?

DISCUSSION

1 One point should be absolutely clear: the two sisters do not experience the event identically. Ursula is certainly 'frantic with opposition and hatred of Gerald' (IX.170). But Gudrun's responses are quite different, and they are described in phrases that don't yield their meanings quite so readily:

> Gudrun was looking at him with black-dilated, spellbound eyes . . . It made Gudrun faint with poignant dizziness, which seemed to penetrate her heart . . . (IX.169).

> The world reeled and passed into nothingness for Gudrun, she could
> not know any more . . . (IX.170)

> Gudrun was as if numbed in her mind by the sense of indomitable soft
> weight of the man, bearing down into the living body of the horse; the
> strong, indomitable thighs of the blond man clenching the palpitating
> body of the mare into pure control . . . (IX.172)

These phrases clearly contradict Leavis' assertion that we are left 'in
no doubt' of the sisters' mutual disapproval. Gudrun's response is in
fact quite different from Ursula's, and seems to me not a moral
response at all. It will perhaps have reminded you of the 'strange
transport' that seized her when she saw Gerald at the wedding
(*Women in Love*, I.61–2; see above, pp. 6–7). The experience at
the level crossing is certainly not an ordinary rapture of pleasure at
the sight of one who is found attractive and admirable: some of the
language even suggests unpleasant symptoms of illness – 'faint', 'dizziness'. But the 'dizziness' is also 'poignant', a sensation that seems to
'penetrate her heart'; she is 'spellbound', captured and fascinated by
the image of Gerald controlling the mare. Her transport is overtly
sexual ('the strong indomitable thighs of the blond man clenching
the palpitating body of the mare') and represents an ecstasy of
admiration for masculine strength, power, domination: a 'fascist'
emotion.

This description could easily be taken for the stuff of cheap
romance, in which palpitating submissive women are always represented as being eager to be dominated by cruel, powerful men.
Does it seem to you to operate like that?

DISCUSSION

If Gudrun is identifying with the mare, it is not (like Ursula) in a passion of 'opposition', but in a masochistic lust to be violated and mastered. Does it seem likely to you that this particular woman is a candidate for such queasy emotions? We already know that Gudrun is
no passive and docile female craving for submission: and it becomes
even clearer as the narrative progresses, that her identification is
rather with the violent cruelty of the man than with the frantic struggles of the victim. Is her challenging remark to him – 'I should think
you're proud' – a rebuke, or a tribute? And does Gudrun submit to
that 'pride', or envy it and covet it for herself? Either way, the reactions of the two sisters need to be sharply distinguished. (My
remarks about 'romance' should perhaps be qualified, since the

language of the novel *does* have a definite relationship with *Romanticism*, which will be considered presently – see below, p. 49ff.)

Furthermore, as you should have noticed, the sisters' respective points-of-view aren't the only narrative perspectives available: the scene is also observed through the eyes of the signalman and of the guard, two neutral and detached observers:

> The one-legged man in the little signal-hut by the road stared out from his security, like a crab from a snail-shell . . . (IX.168).

At one point Gudrun (herself, remember, an artist) visualizes the scene from the guard's perspective:

> And, through the man in the closed wagon, Gudrun could see the whole scene spectacularly, isolated and momentary, like a vision isolated in eternity. (IX.170)

The significance of the scene as an isolated moment, an aesthetic phenomenon, seems to have little to do with moral judgement. The signalman resolutely refuses to moralize or judge:

> 'A masterful young jockey, that; – 'll have his own road, if ever anybody would' . . . the man shook his head, as if he would say nothing, but would think the more. 'I expect he's got to train the mare to stand to anything . . . (IX.171)

The narrative thus offers not one, but three distinct views of the event: Ursula's passion of opposition; Gudrun's perverse sadomasochistic ecstasy; and the signalman's detached, objective perspective which refuses to evaluate or condemn.

You might still, nonetheless, find yourself in broad agreement with Leavis, despite his technical errors. You might feel that the treatment of the mare is *described* in such a vivid way that it *forces* us to recognize Gerald's action as brutal ill-treatment. Can it be anything other than cruelty and violation to force an animal against its natural instincts to face something intolerably terrifying? Doesn't Gudrun simply condemn herself in our eyes by validating, even admiring Gerald's cruelty? If we react in this way, then the art of the novel is, as Leavis insists, pushing us towards Lawrence's own beliefs: the imposition of the power of will over natural instinct is an evil. Such a phrase as 'the mare rebounded like a drop of water from hot iron' – could be adduced as a perfect poetic embodiment of the destructive clash between nature and the machine. And where do those phrases of disapprobation – 'it was a repulsive sight', 'like a disgusting dream that has no end' come from? Are they the sentiments of the characters, or authorial interventions?

2   Most critics have been satisfied with this interpretation. I think it

much more difficult to arrive at a consistent moral evaluation when opposite points-of-view are dramatized with equal clarity and vividness. If Ursula acts as a polarization of *moral*, oppositional attitudes, Gudrun is a focus for emotions of engaged acquiescence. The reader has an equal opportunity to admire Gerald's qualities, as to condemn them. Gerald's 'glistening' power of 'mechanical relentlessness', 'calm as a ray of cold sunshine', is conveyed as powerfully as the mare's convulsions of horror. And how should we react to the language describing Gudrun's fascination? With moral disapprobation? Or with irresistible, though perhaps unpleasant and disturbing, emotional excitement?

> Gudrun looked and saw the trickles of blood on the sides of the mare, and she turned white. And then on the very wound the bright spurs came down, pressing relentlessly. The world reeled and passed into nothingness for Gudrun, she could not know any more.   (IX.70)

The image of gratuitous, unnecessary, *wilful* torture is clear enough. But how should we respond to Gudrun's emotions? Is she blasted and annihilated into 'nothingness' by revulsion? Or is she rather thrown by an extremity of sensation

> ultimate, *physical* consciousness, mindless, utterly sensual . . . (VII.133)

into a state of unconscious fulfilment –

> when the mind and the known world are drowned in darkness –
> . . . then you find yourself a palpable body of darkness, a demon – '
> (III.93).

Can you recall the source of those quotations?
They are both spoken by Birkin: when he is arguing with Hermione, and when he is defining for Gerald the quality of the West African statuette in Halliday's flat. In both cases, Birkin seems to be describing *as desirable* a state very much like Gudrun's at the level-crossing: 'the extreme of physical sensation, beyond the limits of mental consciousness' (VI.127), 'so sensual as to be final, supreme' (VII.133). In the face of connections like this, Leavis' moral polarizations seem to me to break down.

The key problem in 'Coal-Dust', and the point where Leavis' analysis oversimplifies, is the difficulty involved in interpreting and evaluating the language Lawrence employs to describe Gudrun's sensations. In some kinds of writing such experiences of intense physical sensation, in which the mind is temporarily suspended in a torrent of extreme emotion, are regarded as desirable rather than condemned.

Women in Love employs a whole vocabulary of words describing states of dissolution, disintegration, corruption, degradation, putrescence, reduction, decay. From the moralistic view propounded by Leavis, these qualities can only appear negative and undesirable, diametrically opposed to their antitheses: 'the goodness, the holiness, the desire for creation and productive happiness' (XIX.330; see above p. 44 and endnote). But much of this vocabulary of dissolution is drawn from a traditional word-stock, embodied in a linguistic context – that of English Romantic poetry – in which the words are not simply regarded as negatives, signals for moral rejection. If it is possible for a reader to receive this language of corruption *without* an automatic mechanism of moral disapprobation, that fact would subvert some of Leavis' basic premises.

A strikingly different view of the novel has been proposed by Colin Clarke in his book *River of Dissolution*[6], which took issue particularly with what Clarke regards as the simplistic moralism of Leavis' approach. Clarke's argument is based on the view that the literature of Romanticism acknowledged the presence in nature of both productive and destructive energies: and insisted that the destructive should be admitted as an organic part of the whole process of creation and development. Shelley's *Ode to the West Wind* ('Destroyer and Preserver') is a classic statement of this paradoxical reverence for the duality of nature.[7] The recognition could be taken further: if destruction is as much a necessary and valid dimension of life as creation, why not accord to the negative power the same respect, reverence, even admiration, bestowed on the positive? Most mythologies and religions have incorporated worship of the destructive and death-dealing aspects of the world into their fables and rituals; and many treatments of even the Christian theology (such as Milton's *Paradise Lost*) have expressed an ambiguous respect for the powers of darkness.

Give a careful reading to *Women in Love*, Chapter XIV ('Water-Party'), pp. 238–40, from 'Do you smell this little marsh?' to 'I only want us to *know* what we are', and consider the following questions.

1   How does Birkin see the relationship between the 'dark river of dissolution' and the 'silver river of life'?
2   Do you think Birkin is voicing the author's opinions? How does Ursula's reaction affect your reception of his ideas?
3   Which of the two critical opinions we've been looking at, Leavis' or Clarke's, seems best adapted to elucidating this passage?

DISCUSSION

1   The two processes of creation and dissolution are seen as opposite but dialectically inter-related: both equally necessary to the life
and health of nature and humanity. Birkin is describing a *universal*
process: and he asserts that the destructive stream becomes dominant when the creative stream 'lapses': 'the first spasm of universal dissolution' produces the sinister, decadent beauty of 'fleurs du mal'[8]:
'pure flowers of dark corruption', which include Gudrun and Gerald,
perhaps ('in part') Birkin and Ursula themselves. The river of dissolution leads to the end of the world: pursuing their darker impulses,
human beings will eventually annihilate themselves. But Birkin
scarcely regrets this prospect, even welcomes it: since it heralds the
birth of a 'new cycle of creation', (XIV.239). It is in this way that corruption can be seen not only as a necessary element of life, but as the
positively vital activity of the age: if the old world has outlived its
creative potentiality, the forces destroying it are the forces of life and
health, since they are the harbingers, the creators even, of the 'new
cycle'.

2   Whether or not Birkin is acting directly as author's spokesman,
his theory of creation and dissolution certainly reflects Lawrence's
own dualistic philosophy. Compare the passage from the novel with
two other extracts recording Lawrence's thinking: the first from a
biographical memoir by Catherine Carswell; the second from an
essay by Lawrence, 'The Reality of Peace'.

(a)   When he gave me the manuscript [of *Women in Love*] to read, I
      asked him why must he write of people who were so far removed
      from the general run, people so sophisticated and 'artistic' and
      spoiled, that it could hardly matter what they did or said? To
      which he replied that it was only through such people that one
      could discover whither the general run of mankind, the great
      unconscious mass, was tending. There, at the uttermost tips of
      the flower of an epoch's achievement, one could already see the
      beginning of the flower of putrefaction which must take place
      before the seed of the new was ready to fall clear. I gathered too
      that in the nature of the putrefaction the peculiar nature of an
      epoch was revealed. And the more quickly we recognized and
      accepted the nature of the failure, the more speedily would the
      new unknown seed find a condition for its germination. Achieve-
      ment carried to its furthest limits coincided with putrefaction.
      Those who sought the new must take their stand right in the flux.[9]

(b)   We are not only creatures of light and virtue. We are also alive in
      corruption and death. It is necessary to balance the dark against
      the light if we are ever going to be free. We must know that we,

ourselves, are the living stream of seething corruption, this also, all the while, as well as the bright river of life. We must recover our balance to be free. From our bodies comes the issue of corruption as well as the issue of creation. We must have our being in both, our knowledge must consist in both.

. . . It is the bread of pure creation I eat in the body. The fire of creation from out of the wheat passes into my blood, and what was put together in the pure grain now comes asunder, the fire mounts up into my blood, the watery mould washes back down my belly to the underearth. These are the two motions wherein we have our life. Is either a shame to me? Is it a pride to me that in my blood the fire flickers out of the wheaten bread I have partaken of, flickers up to further and higher creation? Then how shall it be a shame that from my blood exudes the bitter sweat of corruption on the journey back to dissolution: how shall it be a shame that in my consciousness appear the heavy marsh flowers of the flux of putrescence, which have their natural roots in the slow stream of decomposition that flows for ever down my bowels?

There is a natural marsh in my belly, and there the snake is naturally at home. Shall he not crawl into my consciousness? Shall I kill him with sticks the moment he lifts his flattened head on my sight? Shall I kill him or pluck out the eye which sees him? None the less, he will swarm within the marsh.

Then let the servant of living corruption take his place among us honourably.[10]

In the passage from the novel and in that from the essay, we find the same insistence on a need to acknowledge these antithetical but twinned processes; and in particular to accept the 'real reality' of the destructive, death-tending stream of corruption and dissolution. We find in both the same series of antitheses: the 'marsh' or 'black river' is opposed to the 'silver river' or 'bright eternal sea'; the 'phosphorescent' beauty of marsh-born creatures, lily and snake, is contrasted with the 'warm, flamy' rose; the 'stream of synthetic creation' polarizes the 'flowering mystery of the death process'; the 'fire of creation' is juxtaposed against 'the flux of putrescence'. Lawrence himself, in extract (b), offers a relatively straightforward account of the duality of nature: the expulsion of excrement is as integral a part of living as the production of energy. Human beings should therefore be prepared to embrace and comprehend both processes as equally constitutive of their paradoxical nature. Birkin's argument in the novel is more philosophical, and echoes the remarks Lawrence made to Catherine Carswell. There he explains that the significant individuals of contemporary society could be distinguished by the degree of their 'putrefaction': since this was the necessary precursor of fresh development, the 'seed of the new'. Those Lawrence regarded as responsible for exploring and discovering the source of the 'new' (such as himself), 'must take their stand right in the flux'.

It should also be emphasized here that Birkin is not as dogmatically certain about his arguments as he frequently appears: he is not sure whether he and Ursula should be ranked as 'fleurs du mal' or not; and he has a nostalgia for 'pure creation' – 'a dry soul is best' (XIV.239). And again we have the interlocutor operating as an inhibition on the unimpeded transmission of Birkin's ideology: Ursula resists his conclusions, insisting that they are not true for her, and that Birkin is in fact a 'devil' who himself introduces the hopelessness and destruction he describes.

3   Let us for the moment assume that Birkin's views are designed to be registered as significant, not undermined by Ursula's objections. Do they affect the ways in which we apprehend the art of the novel? One of the characteristic linguistic techniques of Birkin's discourse is to juxtapose a vocabulary traditionally associated with pleasure – 'beauty' – with words more familiarly linked to the ugly or unpleasant: thus 'marsh, darkness, snakes, dissolution, corruption', are placed in incongruous juxtaposition with 'lilies, silver, brightness, angels, flowers, Aphrodite'. Aphrodite, Greek goddess of beauty, becomes in Birkin's mythology (the name means, literally, 'foamborn') a sinister chthonic power: 'the flowering mystery of the death-process' (IXIV.238–9). The effect of these juxtapositions, supported by the persuasive articulacy of Birkin's affirmations, is to press us to revalue our sense of the relationship of these conventionally antagonistic categories. If the process of decomposition is a function of creative growth, why should it not also be regarded as beautiful? These details would thus appear to support Clarke's view of the novel rather than Leavis'.

The prose of this chapter (XIV) continually echoes and re-echoes the language and imagery of Birkin's exposition. The events of the chapter take place on and around the lake at Shortlands; the central incident is the drowning of Diana Crich. Gudrun describes a river-journey (XIV.226) in which London's poor feature as 'carrion creatures' of the Thames mud. Four Chinese lanterns symmetrically oppose birds and flowers to the creatures of the sea-bottom (XIV.241–2). And in his attempt to rescue his drowning sister, Gerald actually makes a voyage to the underworld of the lake-bed, where he discovers a universe of death corresponding to the world of the living: 'Why come to life again? There's room under that water there for thousands' (XIV.251). It is in the course of Gerald's unsuccessful attempt to rescue his sister, that Gudrun has another of her transcendent visions of him:

Then he clambered into the boat. Oh, and the beauty of the subjection of his loins, white and dimly luminous as he climbed over the side of the boat, made her want to die, to die. The beauty of his dim and luminous loins as he climbed into the boat, his back rounded and soft – ah, this was too much for her, too final a vision. She knew it, and it was fatal. The terrible hopelessness of fate, and of beauty, such beauty!

He was not like a man to her, he was an incarnation, a great phase of life. She saw him press the water out of his face, and look at the bandage on his hand. And she knew it was all no good, and that she would never go beyond him, he was the final approximation of life to her. (XIV.248–9)

The prose employs a technique of incongruous juxtaposition similar to Birkin's: 'beauty, such beauty, white, luminous, soft, incarnation' are confronted by 'subjection, die, fatal, terrible, hopelessness, final'. Gudrun does not experience Gerald, clambering up out of the marshy water, as beautiful *in spite of* the circumambient emotions of fatality, despair, death. The intensity of her sensuous vision is in fact *dependent* on Gerald's proximity to the 'dark river of dissolution' (XIV.238); the beauty she admires, 'white and dimly luminous' is precisely what Birkin calls 'our white phosphorescent flowers of sensuous perfection' (XIV.238). The language used here could be described as a poetic embodiment of Birkin's philosophy: death is experienced as intense beauty, birth and destruction ('incarnation' and 'too final a vision') are fused in a poetry of 'destructive creation'. The power of the language is supported not just by Lawrence's deployment of Romantic language, but also by the validating effects of Birkin's propositions. There is certainly no justification, it seems to me, for attempting (as Leavis does) a clear and final distinction between the creative and the destructive, the morally healthy and the decadent; Birkin on the one hand and Gudrun and Gerald on the other.

I'd like you to recall however the element of hesitancy in Birkin's exposition, in order to keep open another possible direction of interpretation. It can be argued (though we need the evidence of later parts of the novel to do so) that Birkin is *at this stage* still closely involved with the decadent tendencies of his society (consider his relationship with Hermione, not completely broken off until Chapter XXIII, and his position amongst the Breadalby intelligentsia, VIII.146–7); but in the process of extricating himself from them. His celebration of corruption and the dark powers could be regarded as a vestigial symptomatic decadence he is later to shed. I am anticipating important passages in Chapter XIX ('Moony'), especially pp. 330–2, and Chapter XXIII, ('Excurse'), p. 391, where the problem is thoroughly explored. In other words Leavis' moralistic distinction is not necessarily invalidated by the fact that Birkin *at this stage* appears if anything more decadent and absorbed in dissolution than Gerald or Gudrun. You might consider a comment on this question from Keith Sagar, a follower of Leavis:

> But the imagery so far associated with Birkin ('underworld', 'dark', 'inhuman', 'demoniacal', etc.) seems much nearer to Gudrun's world than Ursula's. To some extent the fact that Birkin had felt obliged to use this kind of imagery indicates the extent to which he was himself caught up in the destructive process until Hermione's crushing blow jolts him free of the old world, the old ethic. His new-found self-sufficiency is a necessary starting-point for a healthy approach to human relationships. Afterwards, he 'knew where he belonged', and could return to the world without being drawn into its madness, implicated in its purposes and values.[11]

I'd like you now to return to Chapter IX ('Coal-Dust') and re-read the latter half of the chapter, from p. 173 'The two men stood quite still . . .' to the end. Consider the following questions, using the critical extracts to assist you.

1 The little episode of the two workmen is used to introduce the passage that follows, about Gudrun's relationship with the mining community. What's the link? What do you think of the two men, and their different responses?
2 Do you find evidence in the language of the kind of beauty/ugliness juxtapositions I've been describing in the preceding pages?
3 What attitude do you feel the reader ought to adopt towards Gudrun's 'nostalgia' for the industrial community?

   (a) The glamour and potency, coupled with callousness and mechanism, refer us to Gerald; the underworld voluptuousness and prurience to Minette [Pussum]; the mindless, inhuman, demoniacal, *nostalgic* desire, to the obscene carving at Halliday's. Beldover is as much a part of the underworld as Bohemia. For this is the quality of a whole civilization, and all who subscribe to it are damned. (Keith Sager, 1966)[12]

   (b) The machine takes over something of the age-old glamour of coal, and its mysterious cruelty is half-sanctioned and half repudiated. If Gudrun, suffering from her fascination and resisting, is nevertheless compelled by the callousness and disruptiveness, this is a token of her vitality as well as of something worse. And if the colliers are half-automatized, it is also true that the dark, disruptive force which they mediate is an elemental life-energy . . . At every level the language insists on the continuity between the dis-ruptive energies of the mining community and

the co-ruptive energies of the marsh. And further, we are no more
disposed to a purely negative appraisal or dismissive judgement
in this case than we were in the other.   (Colin Clarke, 1969)[13]

DISCUSSION

1   Do you find the men as 'sinister' as Gudrun does? Is there something coarse, brutal and repulsive about the older man with the
'prurience' of his unabashed sexual appetite? Women don't always
find it pleasant to be lusted after in the street. Perhaps: but isn't there
also something almost idealistic, a genuine commitment to physical
desire, in the older man's insistence that the value of physical passion
transcends the value of money? And isn't there something feeble and
humiliating about the younger man's inhibition and calculating caution? Either way, the episode introduces us to a passage in which
attraction and repulsion are closely intermingled.
2   The whole passage is clearly a sustained juxtaposition of poetic
contrasts: the vocabulary of light, beauty and desire; the language of
darkness, ugliness, mechanical inhumanity. Many phrases operate as
vehicles for the immediate linking of incongruities: 'ugliness overlaid
with beauty', 'foul kind of beauty', 'glamorous thickness', 'potent
and half-repulsive', 'voluptuous resonance of darkness', 'fatal
desire', 'distorted dignity', 'strange glamour', 'strange, nostalgic
ache of desire'. All the terms can be ranged into opposed categories:
'ugliness, black, squalor, foul, thick, machines, cold, iron, disruptive,
fatal, callousness, uncreated, strange, distorted, unnatural, intolerable, impersonal, destructive, power, rottenness', are set into
antagonism with 'beauty, rich, light, warmly, magic, glowing, attraction, caressing, glamorous, potent, voluptuous, vigorous, desire,
dignity'. Some words diffuse ambiguously across the two categories:
'nostalgia, narcotic, spell'.
3   Keith Sagar's comment acknowledges that the prose requires
contradictory responses from the reader: 'glamour and potency,
coupled with callousness and mechanism'; but the moralistic conclusion he draws is strikingly single-minded – 'all who subscribe to it are
damned'. Perhaps the elements of attractiveness are inserted into the
description merely to signify Gudrun's hopeless absorption into the
'flux of putrescence': the concluding paragraph (IX.177) does
suggest that her overpowering emotion is repulsion, and that the
'glamour' of the district casts a powerful, sinister 'spell' over her. But
surely in order to receive the prose as singularly condemnatory,
wouldn't we have to discount the value of half its discourse? Colin
Clarke's analysis seems to me more appropriate: if we apprehend the

writing as both beautiful *and* ugly, then our reaction to it should be correspondingly complex, without any merely negative or dismissive response. I'm not sure if Clarke's analysis is wholly satisfactory: since he seems to want to sustain clear distinctions between 'vitality' and 'something worse', between 'automatization', and 'elemental life-energy', while insisting on a continuity of language connecting them. There still remains, it seems to me, a stress of tension between the contradictory elements of the novel's discourse which makes the act of reading a disturbing as well as exciting experience. The reader who responds with equal intensity to the attractive *and* the repulsive aspects of the writing, is being faced – as Gudrun is – with emotional contradictions that are not easy to resolve.

Read and consider Chapters X and XI ('Sketch-Book' and 'An Island'), in the light of the preceding discussion. Make a note of any details that connect with the ideas, imagery and language we have already encountered. Think also about the following passage from Keith Sagar's book, and decide whether you think it an appropriate and helpful comment. How clearly are the two relationships distinguished? Is there any definite moral adjudication between them?

> The next chapter 'Sketch-Book' translates the same themes into new symbols of disintegration, *fleurs du mal* . . . Set against this is a passage embodying the health, vitality, purity and colour of Ursula's world and life . . . The butterflies are 'a sign that pure creation takes place' (XI.189). Their very distinctiveness and selfhood constitutes a heaven of existence, for transcending the uncreate mess of mud from which life struggled all those aeons ago. Gudrun's *nostalgia de la boue* is a symptom of her unconscious desire to lapse back from the struggle for selfhood towards man's first slime.   (Keith Sagar, 1966)[14]

DISCUSSION

The opening paragraphs of Chapter X certainly seem to distinguish symmetrically and schematically between the two sisters, almost in terms of Birkin's distinction between the 'dark river of dissolution' and the 'silver river of life'. But is there any suggestion of a *moral* distinction within the narrative itself; any indication that we should evaluate the two states of consciousness differently? The prose seems to me equally vivid and compelling in each case: Gudrun's 'sensuous vision' of phallic vitality in the marshy world of mud and water-plants, is as real, complete and interesting an experience as Ursula's rarified absorption into the butterfly-world of 'pure, ethereal sunshine' (X.178). If Gudrun's vision is partial and distorted, so is Ursula's. If the reader is repelled by the turgid energies of the marsh, then presumably he/she is reading in terms of a 'consistent moral scheme' quite out of sympathy with the novel's design or the author's philosophy.

Gudrun encounters Gerald in the midst of this lurid, succulent underworld: the language of her emotion mingles the corruptive fire of the marsh and the disruptive powers of industry:

> And as if in a spell, Gudrun was aware of his body, stretching and surging like the marsh-fire, stretching towards her, his hand coming straight forward like a stem. (X.179)

> And instantly she perished in the keen *frisson* of anticipation, an electric vibration in her veins, intense, much more intense than that which was always humming low in the atmosphere of Beldover. (X.178–9)

The emotional exchanges are again articulated in that Romantic language of dying, fainting, swooning with pleasure, which as we have seen seems designed to produce a troubling and ambiguously exciting, if not wholly enthusiastic, response:

> Her voluptuous, acute apprehension of him made the blood faint in her veins, her mind went dim and unconscious. And he rocked on the water perfectly, like the rocking of phosphorescence. He looked round at the boat. It was drifting off a little. He lifted the oar to bring it back. And the exquisite pleasure of slowly arresting the boat, in the heavy-soft water, was complete as a swoon. (X.179–80)

There is certainly nothing like this in the meeting of Ursula and Birkin. They also meet by the water, but their experience seems unaffected by the proximity of the symbolic 'marsh'. Nor is there any association with the world of industry: Birkin adopts a stance of alienated bitterness towards the social world, and again professes a preference for 'a world empty of people' (XI.188). But there are similarities too. Both relationships seem to involve an unusual intensity of conflict:

> He watched her with an insight that amounted to clairvoyance. He saw her a dangerous, hostile spirit, that could stand undiminished and unabated. (X.181)

> They were rousing each other to a fine passion of opposition . . . it was this duality in feeling which he created in her, that made a fine hate of him quicken in her bowels. (XI.190)

Apparently conflict occurs both in the 'heaven of existence' occupied by Birkin and Ursula, and in the 'uncreate mess of mud' wallowed in by Gerald and Gudrun (see Sagar, above p. 56).

Do Birkin and Ursula nevertheless seem to stand for 'health, vitality, purity' – their conflict only the growing pains of their creative mutual salvation? Birkin certainly wants to create something – but only through destruction of everything that is:

> But I abhor humanity, I wish it was swept away. It could go, and there would be no *absolute* loss, if every human being perished tomorrow. The reality would be untouched.   (XI.187)

Ursula resists and criticizes Birkin's pronouncements: 'Ursula could not help stiffening herself against this' (XI.186); 'she was dissatisfied with *him*' (XI.188); 'Of course, it was only a pleasant fancy' (XI.188); 'Your world is a poor show' (XI.190). But is Ursula resisting Birkin's apocalyptic misanthropy in the name of Sagar's 'health, vitality, purity', or of Leavis' 'goodness, holiness, desire for creation and productive happiness'? If anything, Ursula is more thoroughly committed to the nihilistic doctrine of destruction than Birkin is. What she objects to is not that he believes in the virtues of destruction, but rather that his belief is qualified by a residual affection for humanity:

> She herself knew only too well the actuality of humanity, its hideous actuality. She knew it could not disappear so clearly and conveniently.   (XI.188)

Ursula does not question the principle of such a final solution; in fact she reinforces it:

> And really it *was* attractive: a clean, lovely, humanless world. It was the *really* desirable.   (XI.188)

What Ursula 'mistrusted' and 'hated' were the residual vestiges of Birkin's compassion and human responsibility – that 'final tolerance' which would keep him trying to save the world. Ursula emerges from this dialogue as more committed to the philosophy of annihilation, more deeply steeped in the knowledge of destruction, than Birkin is; 'Her subtle, feminine, demoniacal soul knew it well'; ' "But man will never be gone," she said with insidious, diabolical knowledge of the horrors of persistence' (XI.188).

Please read Chapter XIII ('Mino') and consider the following questions, using the critical extracts as a guide. (The central issue here will be discussed again – see Chapter Four, pp. 79–81, and Chapter Six, pp. 84–90).

1   What kind of relationship is Birkin offering to Ursula, and what do you think of his methods of courtship?
2   Does Ursula resist because she wants to sustain a more conventional relationship? Does she get her way in the end?
3   What is the function in the chapter of the 'fable' of the cats?

DISCUSSION

1 Birkin's statements, though couched in esoteric language, amount to an intelligible and not at all unreasonable aspiration. A relationship of 'equilibrium, a pure balance of two single beings' is surely an attractive possibility. But I expect you can also appreciate Ursula's dissatisfaction with a man who theorizes relationships to such a degree of abstraction.

2 Ursula's questions are very pointed and perceptive: her insight is that Birkin's 'passionate insistence' (XIII.217) springs from insecurity: 'You don't trust yourself. You don't fully believe yourself what you are saying. You don't really want this conjunction, otherwise you wouldn't talk so much about it, you'd get it' (XIII.216). Her resistance draws attention to Birkin's contradictory position: he preaches individual freedom and equality, yet demands from Ursula an elaborate and final pledge; he seems to be resisting his own feelings of love in the interest of clarifying his theory: 'She interpreted it, that he had made a deep confession of love to her. But he was so absurd in his words, also' (XIII.210).

Critics have differed considerably in their reactions to this passage. Leavis for example seems to feel that the position Birkin is arguing for is clearly and unexceptionably correct:

> Ursula, when she asks for love, means the love that could, and should, be 'perfect' and remain that till death. But not only does Birkin recoil from the implicit self-commitment to utter intimacy, and the other falsities and impossibilities; he knows that he must get Ursula to recognize for what it is the inherent matriarchal drive that, obstinately, innocent, takes cover in the feminine devotion to 'perfect love'.[15]

Leavis' revealing phrase, 'he knows that he must get Ursula to recognize', indicates that the critic has an implicit sympathy with Birkin's ideas, and an acquiescence in Birkin's willed persistence. Have those (perhaps unconscious) predilections prevented the critic from apprehending the full range of suggestions offered by the narrative?

Stephen Miko on the other hand is more impressed with Ursula's insight and with Birkin's insecurity:

> Ursula, who still wants an old-fashioned sort of romantic love, interprets all this as a form of selfishness, as a plea for masculine supremacy ... Birkin is very earnest, and this makes Ursula uncomfortable; so it would make us, if Lawrence did not allow her to undercut it repeatedly ... Birkin is once again the petulant child about whom Hermione complained ... Ursula, though too egoistic as well, effectively

reduces Birkin to absurdity by instantly spotting the insecurity under-
lying his insistence. In his awareness of the comedy inherent in Birkin's
overseriousness, Lawrence goes far in meeting the objections that he
is forcing his doctrine down the reader's throat.[16]

Lawrence may well be guilty, Miko implies, of having a 'doctrine':
but the text itself deflects the force of Birkin's arguments by attributing them to his 'insecurity', permitting Ursula to deflate and undercut
them, and introducing a vein of comedy to prick the bubble of
Birkin's earnestness.

3   The fable of the cats is, I think you'll agree, an amusingly ironical
reflection on the human relationship; and a counter to the fre-
quently-stated view that Lawrence was deficient in a sense of
humour. The incident is a beautifully-observed and perfectly-located
subversion of Birkin's authoritarian position, and indeed of the
author's own sexist ideology (see below, Chapter Four, pp. 79–81).
Birkin's application of the example of his own case – it is the desire
to bring this female cat into a pure stable equilibrium' – is surely an
ironical, half-amused confession, and Ursula is quick to seize the
analogy. The victory *is* hers at last; though the 'love' Birkin submits
to remains undefined:

> He stood smiling in frustration and amusement and irritation and
> admiration and love. She was so quick, and so lambent, like discerni-
> ble fire, and so vindictive, and so rich in her dangerous flamy sensitive-
> ness.   (XIII.213).

> He enfolded her, and kissed her subtly, murmuring in a subtle voice of
> love, and irony, and submission: 'Yes, – my love, yes – my love'.
> (XIII.217–8)

The exact nature of Ursula's position is far from clear at this point.
Does she claim Birkin for the cause of traditional romantic love? Or
does she believe his ideal attainable without the renunciation of love?
We shall return to this question in Chapter Six: though you might for
the moment consider the definition of love Ursula (now Mrs Birkin)
offers to Gudrun in Chapter XXIX:

> 'Love is too human and too little. I believe in something inhuman, of
> which love is only a little part. I believe what we must fulfil comes out
> of the unknown to us, and it is something infinitely more than love. It
> isn't so merely *human*'.   (XXIX.534)

Think back now over the contexts and issues we've discussed in these
first three chapters, and list whatever arguments you can remember
which would either substantiate or oppose the Leavisite point-
of-view.

DISCUSSION

For:
1   We have seen that Birkin frequently voices ideas close to Law-
    rence's own philosophy. Although these ideas are articulated
    with reservations and qualifications into a context in which their
    meaning and reception may be modified, Birkin remains the only
    character who expresses a recognizable body of ideas (see above,
    pp. 28–33).
2   Gerald and Birkin are distinguished from one another; the one a
    social conformist, the other an alienated eccentric (*Women in
    Love*, Chapter I); the one a believer in industrial productivity as
    the basis for life, the other an obdurate critic of industrial society
    (*Women in Love*, Chapter V; see above, pp. 29–31).
3   The sisters too are distinguished in Chapter V: with Gudrun
    yearning for Gerald's state of isolation; and Ursula linked with
    the imagery of living plants and growing things (see above,
    pp. 18–20).

Against:
1   If the novel is as 'symmetrical' as Leavis maintains, why did con-
    temporary readers (including himself) encounter such difficulty
    in reading it? (see above, pp. 2–3).
2   Our analysis of the novel's narrative methods should be a caution
    against any attempt to isolate an 'authorial' perspective: since
    clear distinctions between authorial narrative and character-con-
    sciousness are particularly difficult to make (see pp. 3–9).
3   The reactions of readers to Birkin and his ideas are scarcely com-
    patible with seeing Birkin as the author's spokesman. The novel
    uses various devices to inhibit the persuasive effects of his
    speeches (see pp. 31–3).
4   Lawrence's own theory of the novel seems to invalidate any *wil-
    led* didactic content, though he always insisted that we should
    'learn' from the 'art' of the novel, he meant from the 'passional
    inspiration' creating it. Leavis too would have assented to that
    proposition, arguing always that 'great' literature is the spon-
    taneous product of the writer's whole being, never the consequ-
    ence of willed mental impulses (and he criticized Lawrence him-
    self severely when he felt the author had offended against his own
    critical standards; as in *The Plumed Serpent* and *Lady Chatter-
    ley's Lover*.[17] The problem presented by Birkin is that, if we are
    not persuaded by his dogmatic and authoritarian pronounce-
    ments, what else is there to persuade us? (see above, pp. 30–1).

5   Lawrence's concern with 'deeper being', and his use of language
    to reflect the deeper rhythms of experience, would seem to render
    the moral categories Leavis employs redundant. Isn't Leavis
    imposing on the novel precisely the kind of 'consistent moral
    scheme' Lawrence himself explicitly renounced? (see above, pp.
    9–11, pp. 34–41).
6   If you are persuaded by Colin Clarke's interpretation of the novel
    as a genuine *dialectic* of creation and destruction, in which both
    principles are respected or even revered, then it becomes difficult
    to sustain Leavis' moral imperatives. The novel's technique of
    juxtaposing the language of attraction or beauty with that of
    ugliness or repulsion similarly subverts a criticism which seeks an
    absolute separation of 'creativity' and 'dissolution'.

4. Sexual Politics: Homosexuality, Feminism

Women in Love XVIII, XXIV, XXV, XXIX–XXX;
'Prologue' and XX; XIII

This chapter is an attempt to guide you towards some conclusions
about Lawrence's treatment of sexuality in relationships. We will be
re-examining the general comparison and contrast between the
respective relationships of Birkin/Ursula and Gerald/Gudrun; looking at the exploration of homosexual love in the novel, partly by
considering a piece of writing (now known as the 'Prologue' to
Women in Love) intended as part of the novel and discarded before

completion; and considering, from the perspective of feminist criticism, Lawrence's artistic treatment of women.

Why 'sexual politics'? The subject is introduced:

> 'Yes, for example,' cried the Italian. 'That which is between men and women – !'
> 'That is non-social', said Birkin, sarcastically.
> 'Exactly', said Gerald. 'Between me and a woman, the social question does not enter. It is my own affair.'
> 'A ten-pound note on it,' said Birkin.   (VIII.160)

The fact that heterosexuality is a permanent biological necessity for the propagation of the human species makes it a likely candidate for the category of 'unchanging human nature': however extensive the transformations of history, one constitutive human characteristic at least remains the same. The fact that sexual emotions are among the most intense and problematical of individual experiences tends to confirm the sense that they are 'private', detachable from social conventions; and some very influential cultural movements, such as Romanticism, have projected sexual passion as a uniquely transcendent experience on a different plane from the mundane realities of social living.

If we look at sexuality in a historical perspective, such ideas become extremely unsatisfactory. The number of variant forms given to sexual experience – changing conceptions of the erotic and the beautiful, cultural rituals of courtship, forms of the marriage institution, attitudes to divorce, extra-marital sex, adultery, homosexuality – within the history even of our own society – should dissuade us from seeing sexuality as untouched by social and historical factors; and the 'unchanging human nature' idea becomes even less satisfactory if we examine, from the perspectives of sociology or anthropology, the sexual conventions of other societies. A recognition that sexuality and society are interdependent is substantiated by the further acknowledgement that 'individuality' itself is socially conditioned: that, in the words of George Eliot, 'There is no private life that has not been determined by a wider public life'.[1] If the 'social question' *does* in fact, as Birkin sarcastically intimates, enter into the relations between men and women, then any serious and responsible exploration of such relations is incomplete without a consideration of how they are conditioned by society.

A *politics* of sexuality takes this premiss further: it doesn't rest content with an analytical *interpretation* of the connections between society and sexual relations, but insists on the possibility and necessity of a transformation of those relations, which is simultaneously an intervention into the political processes of changing society. A vigorous sexual politics such as that we have today arises when social groups, which have traditionally been subsumed into the ideology of a patriarchal society – women and homosexuals – become conscious, articulate, and determined to reassess and subvert the ideas that hold them prisoner. A *cultural* politics of sexuality involves the re-examination of a society's art on the basis of a conscious intention of resisting the ideologies that work through culture to constitute women as subordinate creatures, or homosexuals as deviant, failed men.

> . . . cultural and political action have become closely united . . . in the women's movement. It is in the nature of feminist politics that signs and images, written and dramatized experience, should be of especial significance. Discourse in all its forms is an obvious concern for feminists, either as places where womens' oppression can be deciphered, or as places where it can be challenged. In any politics which puts identity and relationship centrally at stake, renewing attention to lived experience and the discourse of the body, culture does not need to argue its way to political relevance. Indeed one of the achievements of the womens' movement has been to redeem such phrases as 'lived experience' and 'the discourse of the body' from the empiricist connotations with which much literary theory has invested them. 'Experience' need now no longer signify an appeal away from power-systems and social relations to the privileged certainties of the private, for feminism recognizes no such distinction between questions of the human subject and questions of political struggle. The discourse of the body is not a matter of Lawrencian ganglians and suave loins of darkness, but a *politics* of the body, a rediscovery of its sociality through an awareness of the forces which control and subordinate it.[2]

Eagleton's ironical use of a notorious phrase from *Women in Love* (XXIII.400), 'suave loins of darkness' is an unfortunate dismissal of a writer described by Kate Millett, author of that milestone of feminist cultural criticism, *Sexual Politics* (1971), as 'the most talented and fervid of sexual politicians'[3]. *Women in Love* is very obviously a work of sexual politics: it traces the links between society and sexual relationships; it demonstrates the desirability of some transformation of sexual relationships; it appears to affirm that the fate of society rests on the successful achievement of such transformation. Further, the novel addresses the problem of homosexual love with a remarkable openness (though Lawrence might well have wanted, judging by the 'Prologue', to go further still). Many of Lawrence's *views* on women and homosexuals were notoriously reactionary, and Kate Millett's essay on his writing is partly an ironical de-bunking of the phallic and patriarchal sage: that in itself does not negate the value of the writing as a vehicle for the foregrounding of such central questions. And we will have to consider whether in fact, as Millett argues, the novel preaches a dogmatic 'line' on sexual politics, or operates as a medium for the disclosure and interplay of contradictory attitudes.

Please re-read Chapter XVIII ('Rabbit') and consider the following question:

1   How does the episode with the rabbit function in the dramatization of Gerald and Gudrun's relationship? Is the rabbit itself a 'symbol'? If so, of what?

DISCUSSION

1   The rabbit itself certainly functions 'symbolically', though we would, I think, be hard pressed to say exactly what it symbolizes. On one level, that of vivid naturalistic description, it is quite simply a rabbit: rendered with an acuteness of observation, and a sensuous power of representation, recognizable as characteristic Lawrencian 'strengths':

> It set its four flat feet, and thrust back. There was a long scraping sound as it was hauled forward, and in another instant it was in mid-air, lunging wildly . . . After considering for a few minutes, a soft bunch with a black open eye, which perhaps was looking at them, perhaps was not, it hobbled calmly forward and began to nibble the grass with that mean motion of a rabbit's quick eating. (XVIII.315–18)

At the same time another language is conferred on the rabbit, suggestive of strange powers and demonic possession: 'magically strong . . . demoniacal . . . the long, demon-like beast (315) . . . like a dragon . . . unearthly (316) . . . obeying some unknown incantation (318) . . . mysterious', (319). What possesses the rabbit is at first a frenzy of resistance, perhaps similar to that of the horse in Chapter IX (see above, pp. 45–8); and then a 'fear of death' as Gerald's hand descends on its neck 'like a hawk' (316). Tossed into the walled court, the animal alternates between normal rabbit-like behaviour and a kind of 'madness': 'Round and round the court it went, as if shot from a gun, round and round like a furry meteorite, in a tense, hard circle that seemed to bind their brains' (318). At the end of the chapter, Winifred is 'conjuring' the rabbit as if she were a witch and the animal her familiar: fascinated by the powers it has revealed, she seeks to appropriate them: 'Let its mother stroke its fur then, darling, because it is so mysterious –' (319).

The most important function of the rabbit is, however, to act as a catalyst in arousing and provoking intense emotional responses in Gudrun and Gerald. Gudrun is overcome with 'fury' at its resistance, and Gerald observes in her a 'sullen passion of cruelty' (315). In Gerald the creature's obstructiveness arouses a 'sharp, white-edged wrath' determined to quell its struggles. Both characters are aroused by the rabbit's extremity of terror – a state of pure sensation like the West African statuette's extremity of pain, 'mindless, utterly sensual' (VII.133) – and both are moved by the emotions of cruelty evoked in the other:

> And he saw her eyes black as night in her pallid face, she looked almost unearthly. The scream of the rabbit, after the violent tussle, seemed to have torn the veil of her consciousness. He looked at her, and the whitish, electric gleam in his face intensified.   (XVIII.316)

Just as Gudrun was intensely moved at the sight of Gerald spurring his mare, she responds again with a sado-masochistic ecstasy to his subduing of the rabbit: 'almost supplicating, like a creature which is at his mercy, yet which is his ultimate equal' (XVIII.316–17). Their emotional unanimity involves the excitements of violence and cruelty.

2   Think about the 'Rabbit' chapter in the light of the following crit-ical comments, which seek to define some of Lawrence's episodes as 'ritual scenes' in which characters act out, through significant ges-tures and words, their relationship with the unconscious forces within themselves and to the external forces of their circumambient universe. In what ways is 'Rabbit' a 'ritual scene'?

> *Women in Love* proceeds through a series of counterpointed scenes, which may appear unexpected or random on a strictly realistic level but are inevitable on a deeper, psychic level . . . Thus Gudrun watches admiringly while Gerald brutally subdues the Arab mare at the rail-road crossing in 'Coal-Dust' (IX.168–70). In 'Water-Party' she gives back her challenge by intimidating Gerald's bullocks and striking the 'first blow' (XIV.237). Then in 'Rabbit', they came together as 'in-itiates' while throttling Bismarck. Repeated ritual gestures link the scenes: Gudrun cries out in a voice like a seagull at the critical moments; Gerald's reaction to her challenge in 'Rabbit' echoes that in 'Water-Party': 'He felt again as if she had hit him across the face'. In all three scenes animals stand as symbolic surrogates, dramatic objects towards which the warring partners may direct largely unconscious feelings.   (Charles L. Ross, 1982)[4]

> These scenes are 'rituals' because they dramatize, frequently in solemn ceremonial gesture and in a ceremonious prose, the ultimate relation

of the 'essential' man or woman – usually it is a woman – to what Lawrence calls 'the unknown'. As such they are analogous with religious rites in which the relation of the human soul to God is celebrated. In these scenes the 'old stable ego' of the character shatters, and the individual becomes unrecognizable in his everyday aspect. 'Daytime consciousness' is suspended; the individual is described as coming under the direct influence of irresistible forces of life. Behaviour under these circumstances may be assumed to express an ultimate of the human condition, the inhuman 'isness' of the self. These scenes present an artistic proof that essential being exists and indicate its nature. In them the individual is created anew, in a set of terms distinct from the dramatic and descriptive language used to define the same character as a social being.   (Julian Moynahan, 1963)[5]

DISCUSSION

2   This episode could certainly be described as a 'ritual scene': by means of the 'ritual' of subduing the rabbit, both Gudrun and Gerald experience an ecstasy of violent sensation, defining their passion for each other in terms of the forces of aggression, violence, madness.

The suggestions of 'ritual' in the writing are even more overt than this: Lawrence employs a language of religious ceremony to suggest that the couple are being initiated into a mystery by ritualistic actions and words.

> They were implicated with each other in abhorrent mysteries . . . she looked at him and saw him, and knew that he was initiate as she was initiate.   (XVIII.317–18)

The communion that takes place through this ritual enactment has to be described as 'religious'. Not only does it suggest the invocation of underworld powers: 'Gudrun looked at Gerald with strange, darkened eyes, strained with underworld knowledge . . . He felt the mutual hellish recognition' (XVIII.316–7); it actually brings the characters into contact with some vague, terrifying, non-human power:

> 'What a devil!' he exclaimed. But it was as if he had knowledge of her in the long red rent of her forearm, so silken and soft . . . The long, shallow red rip seemed torn across his own brain, tearing the surface of his ultimate consciousness, letting through the forever unconscious, unthinkable red ether of the beyond, the obscene beyond. (XVIII.317)

The portentous and mysterious language nonetheless conveys a clear and unmistakable meaning. 'Obscene' doesn't vaguely signify 'nasty': it means, literally, that which should never be seen, should be kept hidden by convention and taboo: through the rip in her flesh

Gerald 'knows' Gudrun in a mystical ceremony of ritualized cruelty. 'Ether' (Latin *aether*) means an atmosphere or element: Lawrence employs it to suggest that an intersection takes place here between human experience and an elemental, universal power of violence, 'the beyond, the obscene beyond'.

3 Please read Chapter XXIII ('Excurse'), and note the similarities and differences between the 'strange mystery' of Birkin and Ursula's union (XXIX.395) and the 'mystery' (VIII.317) of 'Rabbit'.

DISCUSSION

3 I expect you felt the *contrast* between 'Rabbit' and 'Excurse' more strongly than anything else. Birkin and Ursula also enter a 'strange element', but is is defined as 'a new heaven' (XXIII.393), a 'paradisal' assumption (XXIII.396). The couple establish contact with some mystical, non-human power – but it is defined as divine rather than diabolical, 'the sons of God from the Beginning' (XXIII.396). There is no emphasis on violence or cruelty, but rather on 'peace' (XXIII.392), immunity from 'stress or excitement' (393), 'rich peace, satisfaction' (396).

But there are similarities too. The fact that both experiences are described as 'religious' communions, though invoking very different supernatural powers, is an important parallel. Birkin is also a 'demon' (XXIII.386) revealing and accepting obscene realities of physical being (XXIII.386). That passage appears early in the chapter, and is perhaps superseded by what follows. But later in the novel the sexuality of their relationship is described in terms curiously similar to those of 'Rabbit':

> Birkin was dancing with Ursula. There were odd little fires playing in his eyes, he seemed to have turned into something wicked and flickering, mocking, suggestive, quite impossible. Ursula was frightened of him, and fascinated . . . troubled and repelled . . . His licentiousness was repulsively attractive . . . She was free, when she knew everything, and no dark, shameful things were denied her.   (XXIX.504–6).

Again the cruelty and violence are absent: but there is an emphasis on the breaking of taboos, the violation of conventional feelings like 'shame' (Birkin and Ursula apparently engage in anal intercourse) which tends to diminish the possibilities for sharp differentiation of two utterly different sexual experiences. 'Excurse' will be discussed at length in Chapter Five (see below, pp. 96–101).

Clearly there is evidence in such a comparison for the Leavisite insistence that the basic 'symmetry of negative and positive' is here observed: that the sexuality of Birkin and Ursula is creative and liberating, that of Gerald and Gudrun destructive and deathly. There is also evidence for the contrary view that the two forms of sexuality are in some ways similar: both perhaps conditioned by the process of degeneration tormenting the society. If the world is coming to an end, as Birkin states again and again, does it make very much difference whether you stand aside from the process or throw yourself into it? I will leave you to consider this further using the critical extracts printed below to assist your thinking.

(a) The main argument of the book, which is the distinction between the 'love' of Rupert and Ursula on the one hand, and of Gerald and Gudrun on the other, is false. Rupert and Ursula are represented as in the way of salvation, Gerald and Gudrun as in the way of damnation: . . . But when we consider the principles which these opposed couples really embody, we discover that the difference between them is that Rupert and Ursula are a whole stage further on in the process of damnation, for Gerald and Gudrun simply represent Rupert and Ursula at their previous stage of sensual self-destruction. (J. M. Murry, 1921)[6]

(b) We are being expected to discriminate between sensual experiences enjoyed by a pair of loving men and women (which are regarded by the novelist as innocently enjoyed) on the one hand, and degenerate indulgences of a society which has cut all connections with spiritual values on the other. (George Ford, 1965)[7]

(c) One cannot even distinguish, discursively, between the sex Gudrun desires from Loerke, which is obscene and decadent, and that which Ursula experiences with Birkin, which is on balance renovatory . . . in practice they presumably amount to almost the same thing . . . Decadence and renovation, death and rebirth, in the last days, are hard to tell apart, being caught up in the terrors. (Frank Kermode, 1968)[8]

Please read and compare three passages: (1) *Women in Love* Chapter XXVII, pp. 458–9; (2) Chapter XXV, p. 440; (3) Chapter XXIX, 510–12. Read passage (2) in conjunction with Chapter XXIV, pp. 430–1. All three extracts deal with marriage. What different conceptions of marriage emerge, and how do they seem to be evaluated, if at all?

DISCUSSION

1 (XXVII.458–9) Ursula quarrels with her father and comes to Birkin. The union that takes place is described as a 'marriage': 'This

marriage with her was his resurrection and his life' (459). This is not however what we normally mean by 'marriage': it is a mystical state of 'oneness' which 'transcended the old existence'. Legal marriage is explicitly differentiated: it happens afterwards as a mere formality: 'They were married by law on the next day . . .' (459). The sexual 'equilibrium' they achieve is defined as independent of social institutions and conventions.

2 (XXV.440). In Chapter XXIV ('Death and Love') the sexual union of Gudrun and Gerald is described in a context of deathliness: he walks directly from his father's grave to Gudrun's bed, the mud of the churchyard still clinging to his boots, as if he were a ghoul or vampire. He comes to her for 'vindication':

> Into her he poured all his pent-up darkness and corrosive death, and he was whole again . . . And she, subject, received him as a vessel filled with his bitter potion of death.   (XXIV.430)

The emphasis on 'bitterness' and 'corrosion', on sexual intercourse as a 'terrible frictional violence of death', seems to distinguish this prose fairly clearly from Lawrence's writing about Birkin and Ursula (though the culmination of their union is also a 'death' – XXIII.399). An even more clearly distinguishing feature is the distance the sexual act creates between the two: while Gerald is healed and soothed by the experience: 'he received of her and was made whole' (430), she is 'destroyed into perfect consciousness':

> She seemed to be hearing waves break on a hidden shore, long, slow, gloomy waves, breaking with the rhythm of fate, so monotonously that it seemed eternal.   (431)

On the basis of *this* kind of sexual relationship, Gudrun and Gerald also, independently of each other, contemplate marriage. To Gerald marriage appears to be a kind of fate or doom:

> He was ready to be doomed. Marriage was like a doom to him. He was willing to condemn himself in marriage, to become like a convict condemned to the mines of the underworld, living no life in the sun, but having a dreadful subterranean activity.   (XXV.440)

Where Birkin and Ursula attain a 'mystic' marriage, subsequently sealed by legal contract, marriage for Gerald is 'a committing of himself in acceptance of the established world', an acceptance of 'the established order, in which he did not livingly believe' (XXV.440). Gerald is conscious that he could never enter a relationship of 'equilibrium' with a woman: Birkin tries to urge him into such a relationship with himself, a 'pure relationship' of equality and singleness with another man, which might then provide a basis for a different kind of intimacy with a woman. Gerald 'could not accept the offer' (XXV.440).

3 (XXIX.510–12). The account of Gudrun's ideas of marriage to Gerald is an important foregrounding of Lawrence's sexual politics. Marriage appears to her an opportunity for the realization of social ambitions. She knows Gerald as a 'perfect instrument', a 'tool' which she could mobilize, to 'solve the problems of the day, the problem of industrialism in the modern world' (510). Her ambitious dreams promote Gerald from mine-owner to Parliamentary minister, a 'Napoleon of peace' who would 'clear up the muddle of labour and industry' (511). But this 'fictitious transport' is destroyed by a 'terrible cynicism' which reveals the futility of the whole social enterprise. Gudrun is aware then that marriage with Gerald involves commitment to a society she regards as dead, a bankrupt mechanism, 'an old, worn-out concern' (512); in ironical cynicism she renounces her dreams. The only reality left to her is the 'perfect moment', the achievement of transient climaxes of emotional intensity:

> 'You be beautiful, my Gerald, and reckless. There *are* perfect moments' . . . It marked one of her supreme moments, the supreme pangs of her nervous gratification. There it was, fixed in eternity for her. (XXIX.512–13)

Please read Chapter XXIX and Chapter XXX, considering the following questions:

1 In what way does the Alpine resort satisfy Gudrun's desire for 'nervous gratification'?
2 What distinction do these chapters make between the two couples?
3 How does the sculptor Loerke fit into the relationship of Gudrun and Gerald? What does she find in him?

DISCUSSION

1 I would settle on passages such as that on p. 492, 'In front was a valley shut in under the sky . . . a shrine, a shadow'. The place offers Gudrun an ultimate intensity of absolute sensation, because it is an 'end of the world': the 'eternal closing-in' (492), a 'great cul-de-sac' of icy finality where the ordinary world reaches its limit. Gudrun's 'strange rapture' is one of arrival: 'she had reached her place'. The experience is absolutely an individual transcendence: Gerald is left behind. The 'navel of the world' is a 'cul-de-sac', dead-end, for him and for their relationship: 'and there was no way out' (492). A similar passage describes Gudrun's 'strange desire' for a 'consummation' among the icy peaks: a final isolation which would also be fulfilment:

'she would be herself the eternal, infinite silence, the sleeping, time-less, frozen centre of the All' (502). Look also at XXIX.514, at Gud-run's 'transfiguration' by the extremity of sensation.

2   Against this we have to set the growing dissatisfaction of Ursula and Birkin with the snow-world of 'frozen eternality' (XXIX.501). Birkin 'couldn't bear this cold, eternal place' without Ursula; after the conversations about art with Gudrun and Loerke (XXIX.517–29) Ursula feels the 'dazzling whiteness' of the 'eternal snow' as hurt-ful: she feels 'doomed . . . as if there were no beyond' (529). The reali-zation that there *is* a way out is a great relief and liberation (530).

3   As the relationship between Gudrun and Gerald becomes a 'com-bat' (506), a contest for supremacy in which one must triumph, she finds in Loerke an alternative route to the satisfaction of her desires. Loerke is a more perfect 'mechanism' than Gerald, having subdued the human more completely to cynical sensationalism:

> To Gudrun, there was in Loerke the rock-bottom of all life. Everybody else must have their illusion, their before and after. But he, with a per-fect stoicism, did without any before and after, dispensed with all illu-sion. He did not deceive himself in the last issue. In the last issue he cared about nothing . . . He existed as a pure, unconnected will, stoical and momentaneous. There was only his work.   (XXIX.521).

Gerald too succeeded in transforming himself into a 'pure and exalted activity' (XVIII.305); but the nature of his work as a director of the great social-productive machine assimilate him to some of the old, illusory beliefs and conventions which Gudrun's cynicism sees through. Loerke, as an aesthete, has succeeded in dispensing with all that, and represents a pure mechanism of human activity, devoid of ethical purpose or moral commitment. His art, on the other hand, accepts and interprets industry, because there is 'nothing but work' – industry is 'serving a machine', art 'enjoying the motion of a machine' (XXIX.519). Art has nothing to do with humanity, emo-tion, morality, or any other humane consideration: it exists for its own sake. Ursula's quarrel with Gudrun and Loerke opposes this aestheticism with a naive truth: 'The world of art is only the truth about the real world' (XXIX.526). Birkin defines Loerke, in terms of his philosophy of the 'river of dissolution', as a chronic case of advanced corruption: 'a little obscene monster of the darkness'. Loerke is not however distanced and dissociated from common humanity in Birkin's eyes: he only represents further stages of the process of degeneration that humanity as a whole is enduring:

> 'But why does anybody care about him?' cried Gerald.
> 'Because they hate the ideal also in their souls. They want to explore the sewers, and he's the wizard rat that swims ahead . . . I suppose you

> want the same . . . only you want to take a quick jump downwards, in a sort of ecstasy – and he ebbs with the stream, the sewer stream. (XXIX.523)

It is Loerke's capacity for extreme corruption that appeals to Gudrun, and promises to take her further than Gerald could:

> What was it, after all, a woman wanted? Was it mere social effect, fulfilment of ambition in the social world, in the community of mankind? Was it even a union in love and goodness? Did she want 'goodness'? Who but a fool could accept this of Gudrun? This was but the street view of her wants. Cross the threshold, and you found her completely, completely cynical about the social world and its advantages. Once inside the house of her soul, and there was a pungent atmosphere of corrosion, an inflamed darkness of sensation, and a vivid, subtle, critical consciousness, that saw the world distorted, horrific. (XXX.549).

Most readers would probably feel that the closing chapters of the novel clarify the distinctions between the two couples to a point where the Leavisite argument for a 'symmetry of negative and positive' seems inescapable. The relationship of Birkin and Ursula survives: Gerald and Gudrun find their fulfilment in a violent conflict which destroys the weaker partner, and Gudrun ebbs away with Loerke down the river of dissolution. But it should perhaps be noted that Birkin and Ursula do only 'survive': they are left at the end of the novel like survivors at the close of a Shakespearean tragedy, picking up the pieces, unable to show with any conviction that a better world is to be established. One condition of our regarding the relationship of Birkin and Ursula as a success is its ability to resolve the contradiction between autonomy and relationship: the couple needs to be a free unit if it is not to be dragged into the process of degeneration; yet if it does not succeed in relating to other human beings, its ultimate success cannot be guaranteed.

> '. . . marriage in the old sense seems to me repulsive. *Égoïsme à deux* is nothing to it. It's a sort of tacit hunting in couples: the world all in couples, each couple in its own little house, watching its own little interests, and stewing in its own little privacy – it's the most repulsive thing on earth'. (XXV.439).

The novel closes with Birkin and Ursula at the Mill, an isolated private couple ('watching its own little interests', perhaps!). The failure of Birkin's relationship with Gerald breaks any connection the independent couple might have had with some co-operative effort of recovery, some concerted attempt to build for a new future. If that future cannot be striven for, why not go down with the ship like

Gerald and Gudrun? We are left at the end with Birkin's 'obstinacy': a very tenuous defence against the cataclysmic collapse of European civilization.

Let us now turn to the subject of homosexuality

Here are two passages by Lawrence on the subject:

> I should like to know why every man that approaches greatness tends to homosexuality, whether he admits it or not: so that he loves the *body* of a man better far than the body of a woman – as I believe the Greeks did, ... I believe a man projects his own image on another man, like on a mirror. But from a woman he wants himself reborn, re-constructed. So he can always get satisfaction from a man, but it is the hardest thing in life to get satisfaction from a woman ... And one is kept by all tradition and instinct from loving men, or a man – for it means just extinction of all the purposive influences.   (1913)[9]

> It is foolish of you to say that it doesn't matter either way – the men loving men ... it matters so much ... to the man himself – at any rate to us northern nations – that it is like a blow of triumphant decay, when I meet Birrell or the others. I simply can't bear it. It is so wrong, it is unbearable. It makes a form of inward corruption which truly makes me scarce able to live. Why is there this horrible sense of frowstiness, so repulsive, as if it came from deep inward dirt – a sort of sewer ... the most dreadful sense of repulsiveness – something like carrion – a vulture gives me the same feeling. I begin to feel mad as I think of it – insane.   (1915)[10]

The intemperate violence of Lawrence's outburst about homosexuality among Cambridge intellectuals sits curiously beside the earlier propositions about homosexual and heterosexual love. Together the two passages express a fundamental contradiction in Lawrence's attitude to homosexuality. It interested him in a speculative way, he often theorized about it in his discursive writings, and he frequently placed homosexual relationships or contacts at important points in his novels. Yet actual homosexuals could provoke in Lawrence paroxysms of horror and repulsion which suggest some degree of imbalance and ambiguity in his approach to the subject. The most obvious and the most common explanation is that Lawrence himself had strong homosexual tendencies which he resisted and suppressed, deflected into aesthetic speculations, and occasionally released in the distorted form of passions of repulsion.

Look at the following passage from the so-called 'Prologue' to *Women in Love*, which concerns Birkin. Does the treatment of homosexual feelings here seem to you paralleled in the novel as it has come down to us? (Consider in comparison *Women in Love*, II.83; XVI.277–8; XX; XXXI.581–3.)

All the time, he recognized that, although he was always drawn to women, feeling more at home with a woman than with a man, yet it was for men that he felt the hot, flushing, roused attraction which a man is supposed to feel for the other sex. Although nearly all his living interchange went on with one woman or another, although he was always terribly intimate with at least one woman, and practically never intimate with a man, yet the male physique had a fascination for him, and for the female physique he felt only a fondness, a sort of sacred love, as for a sister.

In the street, it was the men who roused him by their flesh and their manly, vigorous movement ... Why was a man's beauty, the *beauté male*, so vivid and intoxicating a thing to him, whilst female beauty was something quite unsubstantial, consisting all of look and gesture and revelation of intuitive intelligence? It might be any man, a policeman who suddenly looked up at him as he inquired the way, or a soldier who sat next to him in a railway carriage. How vividly, months afterwards, he would recall the soldier who had sat pressed up close to him on a journey from Charing Cross to Westerham ... And it would seem as if he had always loved men, always and only loved men. And this was the greatest suffering to him.[11]

DISCUSSION

The language of homosexual emotion in the 'Prologue' is more direct and overt than anything in the novel; and it presents Birkin as someone in whom homosexual passions are not only obsessively persistent, but also problematical, since they complicate the man's relations with women. In the novel we now have, Birkin thinks always of 'love' and 'friendship', never of a sexual relationship with Gerald. Early in the novel we are told that 'they burned with each other, inwardly' (II.83); Birkin realizes that he has a need to 'love a man purely and fully' (XVI.277) as well as a woman, and asks Gerald to swear a modern *Blutbrüderschaft*; at the novel's close Birkin feels that Gerald has lost a chance of salvation by refusing his preferred love: 'He should have loved me ... I offered him' (XXXI.581). Had Gerald fully and irrevocably accepted Birkin's contract of friendship, 'death would not have mattered' (XXXI.581); Gerald's end would not have been a 'barren tragedy' (XXXI.577). The chapter 'Gladiatorial' (XX) brings the theme as close as the novel gets to *physical* relations between men: the wrestling episode is another 'ritual scene' in which a close union of physical bodies produces a state of 'mindless, utterly sensual' (VII.133) intimacy; and out of that, the clasp of hands (XX.351) which Birkin later recalls as the potential ground of a true relationship: 'If he had kept true to that clasp, death would not have mattered' (XXXI.581).

In *Women in Love* love between men is always regarded as *complementary* to heterosexual love between man and woman. In the 'Prologue' however, homosexual love is an *alternative* to heterosexual, as if the two are incompatible or at least difficult to adjust one to the other. Study of the manuscripts and typescripts of the novel shows, that at earlier stages of writing Lawrence was thinking of the homosexual relationship as incompatible with the heterosexual; one of the passages Lawrence excised from the final typescript reads:

> Gerald and he had a curious love for each other. It was a love that was ultimately death, a love which was complemented by the hatred for woman ... It tore man from woman, and woman from man. The two halves divided and separated, each drawing away to itself. And the great chasm that came between the two sundered halves was death, universal death.[12]

The idea that male friendship and heterosexual marriage could be irreconcilable opposites would clearly introduce a deep contradiction into the novel, which no amount of ingenuity in the creation of organic form could hope to resolve. George Ford argues that the earlier intention would have produced an impossibly complex denouement, and that Lawrence was right to simplify the issues:

> In *Women in Love* as finally published what Lawrence wanted to explore was the *possibility* of two ideal relationships, that between Birkin and Ursula, with its redemptive effects on the hero, and that between Birkin and Gerald. If the male relationship had been represented throughout the novel as simply corrupting, and as an alternative rather than as a co-ordinate relationship, then Gerald would appear not as a possible friend but as a purely destructive agent ... In the published novel, the friendship with Gerald is not usually represented as rivalling this affirmative love for woman but as a possible complement, a possibility not realized but wistfully longed for by the hero.
> ... If the rejected chapter and other passages had been retained, there would have been a different kind of drama and an even more highly complex novel than we now have. It seems likely that fear of censorship was not the only reason that led Lawrence to abandon his Prologue chapter.[13]

It is perhaps worth considering, while you weigh the value of Ford's comments, whether the novel *has* benefitted from the diminishing of the original foregrounding of a contradictory sexual politics. The novel, had it retained those contradictions, would certainly have expressed Lawrence's contradictory views of homosexuality more completely. It would also have conveyed an even stronger sense of the irreducible difficulty and complexity attending the effort to achieve and sustain sexual relationships of 'equilibrium' and 'freedom'. The changes are not of course damaging in any final sense, as those contradictions remain in the novel, which resolutely foregrounds its incapacity to solve the problems of relationship. But it is worth bearing in mind that the choices and decisions a writer makes in the cause of making a work of art are not invariably to be sanctioned in the light of the finished product as inevitable and correct.

Women in love; an emphasis then on the particular role and experience of the female gender. But women *in love* – with men; women defined as interesting and important only in terms of their relationships with men. Lawrence's writing is of interest to a feminist sexual politics because, like his treatment of homosexuality, it is based on acute contradictions of attitude and ideology: 'Attacks on Lawrence's misogyny and praise for his sensitive portrayals of femininity have co-existed since the inception of the critical debate'[14]. John Middleton Murry was perhaps the first critic to attack Lawrence's writing from a feminist perspective: ↘

> To annihilate the female insatiably demanding physical satisfaction from the man who cannot give it her – the female who has thus annihilated him – this is Lawrence's desire. To make her subject again, to reestablish his own manhood – this is the secret purpose of *Women in Love*. In imagination, he has his desire. He creates a sexual mystery beyond the phallic, wherein he is the lord; and he makes the woman acknowledge the existence of this ultra-phallic realm, and his own lordship in it.[15]

Murry is interpreting the writing as a direct expression of Lawrence's own psycho-sexual problems – inadequacy and impotence – and an attempt to create an idealized resolution in the subjection of Ursula, her forced renunciation of the female will (which Murry understands here as female sexual appetite) and her submission to a dark, ultra-phallic lordship. Such a psychoanalytical approach has its dangers: the value of fiction can't rest only in its rehearsal of the author's hang-ups or its expression of his defensive, self-indulgent fantasies. On the other hand Lawrence did invite such critical attention both by putting so much of himself in his novels, and by preaching the wisdom of his fictions in his personal and public relationships. Murry's arguments formed the basis for Kate Millett's analysis of Lawrence's sexual politics, which we will consider below in more detail.

Millett's essay was attacked in a famous defence of Lawrence's writing on sexuality by Norman Mailer:

> . . . Lawrence understood women as they had never been understood before, understood them with all the tortured fever of a man who had the soul of a beautiful, imperious and passionate woman, yet he was

locked into the body of a middling male physique, not physically strong, of reasonable good looks, pleasant to somewhat seedy-looking man, no stud. What a nightmare to balance that soul! To take the man in himself, locked from youth into every need for profound female companionship, a man almost wholly orientated toward the company of women, and attempt to go out into the world of men, indeed even dominate the world of men, so that he might find a balance.[16]

Mailer's psychoanalysis is perhaps no more satisfactory than Murry's: though he is correct in drawing attention to Lawrence's personal intimacy with women – initially mother and sisters, later many female friends as well as lovers; and to the author's own poor qualifications for the role of *macho* man. Mailer is also a notorious anti-feminist: but female critics too have been unhappy with the Murry–Millett argument. Lydia Blanchard writes:

> Lawrence is the archetypal male chauvinist – that is doctrine now accepted by nearly every current book reviewer, popular critic, and cocktail party pundit, and even those women who admire the way in which Lawrence uses words are quick to add that they feel nothing but contempt for the way in which he uses women.
>
> But to accept Lawrence as a writer whose ideas are anathema for any self-respecting woman – or man – is to misunderstand the canon of his fiction. Lawrence in his life and in his non-fiction, particularly his letters, was certainly capable of spouting much nonsense about not only the subjugation of women but also the subjugation of a good many men, of talking wildly about the establishment of fascistic states and the submission of lesser beings to their superiors. His fiction, however, presents a very different kind of picture, one illuminating for any person seriously interested in exploring the myriad relationships possible between man and woman.[17]

Kate Millett's essay begins with an analysis of *Lady Chatterley's Lover*, devoted to showing that Lawrence was here concerned to subjugate the woman to the dominion of the masculine phallus (237–45). Her survey of the earlier writings repeats Murry's assumption that the fiction is wholly autobiographical, a sustained effort by Lawrence to vindicate himself as male against various attempts at female dominance over him. Below I have reproduced some of the passages from Millett's essay which deal with *Women in Love*. Give a careful consideration to her arguments, checking back her references to the novel, and reminding yourself of earlier discussions of the same illustrations in this guide. What's your view of her arguments and her conclusions? (See above Chapter I, pp. 16–18; Chapter 2, pp. 23–9; Chapter 3, pp. 45–8 and pp. 58–60.

Women in Love presents us with the new man newly arrived in time to give Ursula her comeuppance and demote her back to wifely subjection. It is important to understand how pressing a mission Lawrence conceived this to be, for he came himself upon the errand. The novel, as stated in the preface, is autobiographical [: 'The novel pretends only to be a record of the writer's own desires, aspirations, struggles, in a word, a record of the profoundest experiences in the self']; its hero, Rupert Birkin, is Lawrence himself. Much of the description of Birkin is rendered through the eyes of Ursula who is in love with him, so that expressions of admiration abound; his brows have a 'curious hidden richness . . . rich fine exquisite curves, the powerful beauty of life itself, a sense of richness and liberty' (IV.94), we are asked also to see in him 'the rare quality of an utterly desirable man' (XI.190) which is rather a lot to say of oneself. Birkin is a prophet, the Son of God at last. . . . Ursula is to join Birkin, and the two will be the new couple which according to the official pronouncements and rules which Birkin lays down shall be a perfect equilibrium between polarities, 'a pure balance of two single beings – as the stars balance each other' (XIII.210). This type of surface assertion is betrayed over and over by the obvious contradictions between preachment and practice. One of the book's most dynamic scenes is Gerald Critch's [sic] abuse of a fine Arab mare whom he forces to a railroad crossing, asserting his will in a fashion he fancies is masculine and Birkin finds agreeable, cutting the animal badly in the process. The incident takes on symbolic force as Birkin sermonizes on it, comparing the mare mastered to the woman mastered: 'It's the last, perhaps highest love-impulses – to resign your will to the higher being . . . And woman is the same as horses: two wills act in opposition inside her. With one will, she wants to subject herself utterly. With the other, she wants to bolt, and pitch her rider to perdition' (XII.202).

. . . On the day when Ursula comes to take tea with him and he proposes an alliance with her on the stellar plan, his trump card, and the symbolic explanation of his intentions, turns out to be the object lesson put forward by his cat . . . The 'new' relationship, while posing as an affirmation of the primal unconscious sexual being, to adopt Lawrence's jargon, is in effect a denial of personality in the woman. Birkin is full of opinions and ideas and holds forth all through the book while Ursula puts docile leading questions to him. Though she requires some effort to tame, she comes to follow him in apostolic faith. The separate spheres live on in a smart and new verbiage, but 'the real terms of the contract', a far harsher matter, are supplied by Mino the cat, in his exercise of authority over his inferior mate . . . Ursula draws the parallel, in case we missed it: 'It's just like Gerald Critch [sic] with his horse – a lust for bullying – a real *Wille zur Macht*' (XIII.213). Birkin defends such conduct and brings home the moral: 'With the Mino it is a desire to bring this female cat into pure stable equilibrium' (XIII.213) . . . And of course a star in Birkin's orbit is exactly what Ursula's position is to be; Birkin will play at the Son of God, Ursula revolving quietly at his side.[18]

DISCUSSION

I hope you noticed some of the errors of fact and interpretation which pervade this argument, and almost deprive it of any capacity to convince or persuade. These are the points I would make against Millett:

1   To identify Birkin with Lawrence is an oversimplification: what the preface (actually 'Foreword') says about 'the profoundest experiences in the self' is not an indication that Birkin *is* Lawrence (above, pp. 29–33);
2   The two passages of flattering description (IV.94, XI.190) are juxtaposed with far less flattering characteristics: Ursula sees in Birkin not only 'an utterly desirable man', but also – in the same paragraph – 'a Sunday-school teacher, a prig of the stiffest type' (XI.190) (see above, pp. 17–18);
3   Millett's comments on the horse-episode in 'Coal-Dust' (IX.168–72) imply that Birkin was present, and is later referring to Gerald's cruelty as illustration. In fact Birkin is not there at all, and in the subsequent discussion is talking more about men and women than horses. His views are, of course, chauvinistic and reactionary: Millett might have mentioned that Ursula finds them so – 'Birkin seemed to her almost a monster of hateful arrogance' (XII.203), and shuns him in favour of a temporary alliance with Hermione;
4   The fable of the cats (XIII) is regarded simply as a confirmation of Birkin's patriarchal wisdom. I have defined it as a subversion of his views (see above, Chapter 3, pp. 58–60); but though there is room for disagreement, we ought surely to recognize the presence of contradiction in the text. *Ursula* certainly regards Mino's behaviour as an exposure of Birkin's male chauvinism;
5   Ursula is capable of more than 'docile leading questions'. Millett herself quotes Ursula's definition of Mino's bullying as analogous to Gerald's cruelty: 'a real *Wille zur Macht*' (XIII.213). That sounds to me more like a sophisticated, spirited and articulate argument than a 'docile leading question'.

Millett's comments do nevertheless raise genuine problems about the novel. *Is* Birkin, despite the complexities of presentation, still used as a mouthpiece for Lawrence's own ideas? *Does* Ursula, despite her energetic resistance, ultimately submit to some divine patriarchal power in Birkin? Do Birkin and Ursula achieve the stellar equilibrium the man promises, or does Ursula remain a satellite? It would be a pity if the intellectual poverty of Millett's argument were to be used against the possibility of feminist reading: and I have certainly not been criticizing it to that purpose. It is a greater pity that there is little good feminist criticism on Lawrence; though my 'Suggestions for Further Reading' (p. 136) will tell you what there is. What such an exercise discloses is the inadequacy of an *oversimplified* methodology for explaining the contradictions and complexities of a novel such as *Women in Love*. The novel may contain reactionary views on sexual politics. But it *contains* rather than promotes them; they are simultaneously juxtaposed with contradictory, oppositional attitudes and energies. If the novel introduces contradictions, as Millett inadvertently admits (p. 263), and fails to reconcile them, that is scarcely evidence of the writer's psychological malaise and confusion. For such contradictions, as a feminist would be the first to admit, can be resolved only by political struggle and transformation, not by the reassuring reconciliations of fiction.

A consideration of three different approaches to the sexual politics of *Women in Love* will perhaps point us to rather different conclusions in each case.

1　There is certainly a tendency in the novel to distinguish sharply between the sexuality of two relationships: and we might read that contrast, updating Leavis' arguments, as a political intervention. The sexual relationship, which seeks to retain outdated social forms as its structural framework, is doomed to collapse into emptiness and perversity; that which explores other modes of relationship (Birkin's 'star-equilibrium') independently of social convention, has some possibility of success and mutual fulfilment. An argument of this kind would have to explain why the distinction between the two relationships is so often obscured in the novel; and why Lawrence seems continually to emphasize the surrounding context of a collapsing world in which the fundamental problems of human survival seems to render such distinctions irrelevant. This 'apocalyptic' character of the novel is considered in the next chapter.

2　A comparison of the outspoken language of the 'Prologue' and the more guarded expressions of the novel suggests perhaps that on the subject of homosexuality Lawrence felt unable to speak out freely. Can we infer that he was in favour of some kind of physical relationship between men (symbolized by the wrestling episode, XX) to complement their love for women? If so, the novel doesn't (for whatever reasons) express this explicitly, nor is any similar freedom considered for women. Or was Lawrence rather, considering his pronounced dislike of practising homosexuals, advocating a more general idea of male friendship which isn't what we'd normally

consider homosexual love? Or does the novel simply play out those
contradictory attitudes towards homosexuality between which
Lawrence evidently alternated?

3　I have suggested that good feminist criticism on *Women in Love*
has yet to emerge. I suspect (though perhaps many feminists would
disagree) that a good feminist reading would take into account the
contradictions in the novel's treatment of women: the contrast between bullying, chauvinist men and intelligent, independent women;
the attempts to assert patriarchal dominance and the rebellion of
women against it; the dialectic of masculine oppression and femine
resistance. That play of contradictions – rather than any ideologi-
cally orthodox expression of feminist sentiments – might perhaps
constitute the novel's true value as a potential site for the articulation
of a sexual politics.

5. Metaphysic, Apocalypse

Women in Love, XV–XXIV

Most of the criticism we've looked at so far is based on a *mimetic* or
representational view of literature: fiction presents us with depic-
tions and dramatizations of real-life people and situations whose
moral problems, discoveries and failures mirror and illuminate those
of Lawrence's (and by implication our own) contemporary humanity. The world the novel presents is the world we know: the transformation of reality into art only integrates and subdues life to the
interpretative perspective of a controlling moral consciousness.
Leavis and Colin Clarke, for example, are in fundamental disagreement over many issues, yet they share, ultimately, a mimetic view of
literature: Clarke commends Leavis for having demonstrated that

each of Lawrence's 'great' novels (*the Rainbow* and *Women in Love*) 'mediates a moral–religious vision of experience, communicated through a fully-realized imaginative rendering of life'.[1]

But what exactly is the relationship between this 'fully-realized imaginative *rendering*' and the 'moral– religious *vision*': and are they necessarily balanced or complementary in *Women in Love*? What happens if there is contradiction between that which the imagination renders and that which the vision reveals? Does the vision bend the world to accord with its own shape? Or does the 'rendering' subvert and subordinate the vision? Criticism has an answer to that difficulty. The 'vision' is not an ideology, not a body of ideas existing prior to the execution of the created work: but rather the *product* of the creative work, that which ensues from its 'imaginative rendering'. Vision and rendering become identical. But in practice the two elements need not necessarily cohere in perfect balance: some novels lean much further in the direction of 'rendering', seeking the accurate representation of reality through mimetic naturalism; others place a much stronger emphasis on a structure of ideas, a pattern of traditional narrative or rhetorical devices, or a body of myths, and incorporate their observations of experience into that predetermined framework. To Lawrence and other writers of his period (such as James Joyce and Virginia Woolf) the distinction seemed clear enough: the great Victorian tradition of the realist novel had outlived its usefulness, and was being perpetuated in a sterile, dead-end way by such novelists as H. G. Wells, John Galsworthy, Arnold Bennett. Writers of the 1920s felt that their task was to explore alternative worlds of experience, Lawrence's deep unconscious ego, Joyce's 'stream-of-consciousness', Woolf's subjective impressionism: and in doing so they subverted the traditional claims of realism to a privileged monopoly of accurate representation.[2]

The traditional terminology of literary analysis – description, dialogue, characterization, plot, language – all tend to presuppose the medium of realistic, representational fiction. Such terms become inadequate, as we have seen, when applied to *Women in Love*. 'Character-analysis' is an instrument for evaluating figures which represent real people: Lawrence's new theory of psychology brought to birth creatures of an elusive complexity not amenable to conventional interpretative methods. 'Plot' assumes that a novel is held together by an interaction of cause and effect, and will progress (perhaps through chronological shifts) in a discernible direction, with an inevitable momentum, to a determined end. *Women in Love* substitutes for traditional plot a discontinuous, episodic structure, and a tendency to invoke large-scale, universal processes quite beyond the scope of any rational concatenation of cause-and-effect. In realistic fiction, descriptive and analytical language is employed to represent a society and its inhabitants with a maximum of concrete social reality and vivid psychological detail. Lawrence's prose in *Women in Love* also 'represents', but in an unusual way: not by objective presentation but by a ritualistic enactment of sensory experience designed to secure intense empathetic engagement rather than dispassionate conscious awareness. The 'reality' his prose evokes is not the clear, hard fact of documentary observation, but the intangible, elusive rhythms of emotional reverberation. It is important to observe that we are talking here purely about literary conventions of different types. 'Realist' fiction obviously has pretensions to the accurate representation of 'reality', but modern criticism has grown increasingly suspicious of its claims, increasingly conscious that 'realistic' visions of the world are just as much imaginative constructions as overtly non-realistic ones. 'Post-modernist' literary critics have found it necessary to re-address Lawrence's fiction with methods and perspectives freed from the realist bias: to consider Lawrence's novels not as *mimesis*, the imitation of contemporary reality, but as myth, or apocalyptic type, or prophecy, or religion; to read *Women in Love* as a *visionary* rather than a *realistic* novel.

I want you now to explore some of these implications by consideration of an important central chapter, XIX ('Moony'). The 'visionary' elements of this chapter are more noticeable in its later stages: first I'd like you to work through some exercises focused on the earlier parts of the chapter. Please read Chapter XIX ('Moony'), pp. 320–9 (from the beginning to '. . . he, too, had his idea and his will'). The chapter begins with an account of Ursula's despair, but plunges very rapidly into a densely-written symbolic scene with little orientating context to elucidate it. The symbolic scene of Birkin's stone-throwing is then followed by a relatively realistic dialogue, edging into a quarrel, about domination and subservience in a relationship (much the same theme as the argument in 'Mino'), between Ursula and Birkin. Think about the separate elements of the chapter – opening narrative, symbolic or 'ritual' scene, ensuing dialogue – in their inter-relationship, and consider the following questions:

1   Why does the chapter begin with Ursula? What association are aroused by the application to her of such words as 'luminousness' and 'radiance'?
2   In terms of narrative event, very little happens in this section of the novel: Birkin throws stones at a pond, Ursula asks him to stop, and they resume the quarrel initiated in 'Mino' (XIII). What

is the point of the stoning episode? What does it tell us about the progress of the novel's meaning?

3 Does the subsequent dialogue between Ursula and Birkin (XIX.326–8) clarify the symbolic scene?

(*Note*: Birkin, talking to himself (p. 323), speaks of 'Cybele – . . . The accursed Syria Dea!' – an Asiatic fertility goddess and mother-figure, whose acolytes would mutilate or even emasculate themselves in a ritual 'Day of Blood'.)

DISCUSSION

1 We are drawn into this chapter *via* an emphasis on Ursula, who has arrived at a bedrock of bitter misanthropy: 'She despised and detested the whole show' (XIX.320); her psychological state a contradictory amalgam of love and hate: 'She thought she loved, she thought she was full of love. This was her idea of herself. But the strange brightness of her presence, a marvellous radiance of intrinsic vitality, was a luminousness of supreme repudiation, nothing but repudiation' (XIX.320–1). The words 'brightness', 'luminousness' and 'radiance' inevitably link Ursula with the moon; and Birkin's subsequent mythological mutterings (XIX.323) identify the moon, a pagan mother-figure, and (presumably) the Ursula whose pretensions to be the 'perfect womb' (XXIII.391) he attacks again and again. Some critics interpret the moon as a symbol of Ursula herself: and Birkin's destructive attack on its integral purity an assault on the matriarchal female:

> Birkin . . . hurls maledictions at the moon, calling her Cybele, the accursed Syria Dea; . . . it is clear enough that the moon is the white goddess, the primal woman image, *das ewig weibliche*, by whom he is obviously haunted. He tries to drive her away, but of course she always comes back; as soon as he stops his stone-throwing the moon-image reforms. At this moment Ursula appears . . . (Graham Hough, 1956)[3]

Leavis puts it rather differently, seeing the moon as a symbol of the 'idealized love' that Ursula demands and Birkin (in Leavis' view quite rightly) seeks to destroy:

> . . . the moon that Birkin tries to shatter is Western idealized love, and – inevitably, she having been bred in our civilization – Ursula, when she asks for love, means the love that could, and should, be 'perfect' and remain that till death. But not only does Birkin recoil from the implicit self-commitment to utter intimacy, and the other falsities and

impossibilities; he knows that he must get Ursula to recognize for what it is the inherent matriarchal drive that, obstinately, innocent, takes cover in the feminine devotion to 'perfect love'.   (F. R. Leavis, 1955)[4]

2   When we come to examine the passage of symbolic writing itself, there seem to be sound reasons for such a critical interpretation. Birkin's words do seem to identify moon, Ursula and *Syria Dea*; Ursula feels herself destroyed and shattered: 'She felt she had fallen to the ground and was spilled out, like water on the earth' (XIX.324). The man's attempt to annihilate the moon's reflection is not, of course, successful: it gathers itself together again, 're-asserted, renewed . . . whole and composed, at peace' (XIX.325). Ursula too resists what she regards as the bullying and insistence of both Birkin and her father: by the end of the chapter she is restored to her original hard brightness: 'Recoiling upon herself, she became hard and self-completed, like a jewel. She was bright and invulnerable, quite free and happy, perfectly liberated in her self-possession' (XIX.340). She becomes leagued in a fierce feminist sorority with Gudrun (XIX.340–2) but then withdraws from that connection and leans again towards Birkin – without, however, renouncing her matriarchal demands: 'She believed that love was *everything*. Man must render himself up to her'. (XIX.343).

Let us examine the stoning episode itself more closely. It is worth saying, to start with, that the writing here is of an extraordinary intensity and force. It operates partly by bringing together an incredibly vivid series of visual and sensory impressions – images and sounds – to create what seems a powerfully 'real' imaginative experience. Yet the account is some distance from what we could ever 'imagine' actually happening: Lawrence's prose has constructed something quite unique and unforseeable.

There seem to me three particularly important techniques employed here: a mixing of metaphors, some incongruously juxtaposed; an interplay of light and darkness; and an alternating rhythm of disintegration and reconstruction. The broken moon is compared to a 'cuttle fish' or 'luminous polyp', with 'arms of fire' (323); 'white and dangerous fire' and 'white birds'; a body of fire' (323) which is also 'the heart of the rose' (324). Separate 'elements' (air, fire, water) are confused together, different associations battle for prominence. The unusual juxtapositions make it impossible for the reader to receive the account as a straightforwardly objective description of an event – the moon's reflection dissipating and reforming; the writing is both more disturbing and wider in its range of expression. The explanations of Leavis and Hough seem therefore too simple and reductive: Birkin is attacking something more than a symbol of matriarchy or idealized love.

The interplay of darkness and light as Birkin tries to dissolve the moonlight into shadow, surely echoes the imagery of the two rivers, the 'dark river of dissolution' and the 'silver river of life': 'The furthest waves of light, fleeing out, seemed to be clamouring against the shore for escape, the waves of darkness came in heavily, running under towards the centre.' (323). Birkin seems then to be provoking a conflict between the two universal principles rather than seeking to obliterate one of them. That at least is the product of his efforts, since the moon continually reforms out of chaotic disintegration:

> . . . the rays were hastening in thin lines of light, to return to the strengthened moon, that shook upon the water in triumphant reassumption. (323).

> He saw the moon regathering itself insidiously, saw the heart of the rose interwining vigorously and blindly, calling back the scattered fragments, winning home the fragments in a pulse and in effort of return. (324).

> . . . a distorted, frayed moon was shaking upon the waters again, reasserted, renewed, trying to get over the disfigurement and the agitation, to be whole and composed, at peace. (325).

Each reader is drawn into an imaginative enactment of this dialectical rhythm of dissolution and reconstruction: it would be absurd to suggest that women readers should feel destroyed by this prose, while their male counterparts can identify smugly with the masculine destroyer. The prose is working at a level of sensation and emotional rhythm rather than of rational concept: so that the reader *feels* rather than *understands* its import:

> We experience (as no mere account can convey) a breaking-apart, a smashing fragmentation, to the very last 'broken flakes' of flight. And we experience the coming together, out of that ultimate separation, into moon-equilibrium, polarity, constellation. The moon that had been sinister and deadly in self-sufficiency grows into a radiant rose – incandescent fire constellated in the dark water.[5]

Thus the reader is imaginatively drawn through an *experience* of disintegration and reconstruction, apprehending it at the level of sensory perception. On the basis of this more complex reading, other critics have argued that the scene is more concerned with the 'ego' or 'will', and the need for its destruction, than with specifically matriarchal dominance; thus Colin Clarke writes:

Critics appear to be unanimous that what the scene is centrally about is Birkin's hatred of the Magna Mater, the accursed Syria Dea; in hurling stones at the image of the moon he is reacting in fury against female arrogance – or tyranny, or possessiveness. But the whole scene has much more to do with integration and disintegration, the need to smash the false integrity of the ego in order to make possible the true integrity of the blood . . . So the significance of Birkin's stone-throwing would appear to be clear: it is an attack on that deathly supremacy of the ego that makes for mere separateness and indifference.[6]

In Clarke's view, Birkin is not attacking *female* arrogance as such, but seeking to shatter the tyranny of the ego which afflicts all human beings in his world. Mark Kinkead-Weekes explains it in terms of opposition, which he sees as central to Lawrence's vision:

The darkness and the light are the two fundamental opposites of . . . *Women in Love*. The darkness embodies the world of the senses and the flesh, of the unconscious . . . The moon is the world of . . . Diana, of the self-sufficient woman who needs no man . . . The scene that follows is an answer to the question 'what else is there?'; but it is an answer not in terms of static symbol but essentially in terms of a process, revealing, imaginatively, the way of salvation. This is why one instinctively knows that this is the heart of the novel, against which everything else has to be defined. If we trust ourselves to the fiction, we *experience* an enactment, stage by stage, first of the process of death and rebirth through the marriage of opposites, . . . and then of the whole process of recreation through disintegration. infinite going-apart, that is central to *Women in Love*.[7]

Both Clarke and Kinkead-Weekes reject the argument that Birkin's stoning of the moon represents his assault on matriarchal dominance. Both critics concur in linking the episode to the novel's structural polarity of creation and dissolution, and beyond the novel to a dialectic of integration and disintegration formulated by Lawrence in some discursive philosophical essays written during the early years of the war. In *The Crown* and *The Reality of Peace*[8] Lawrence argued that disintegration is a necessary process which should be acquiesced in, not resisted or arrested: we should permit, even assist, the old and outworn to decay in order to prepare for the growth of the new. In the light of this theory of being, Birkin is not seeking to smash the *female* ego, but the 'false integrity of the ego' which must be fractured before a new integrity based on the whole being can begin to cohere: 'the whole process of recreation through disintegration, infinite going apart'.

3   Which of these two views seems to be supported by the dialogue between Ursula and Birkin that follows the stoning episode? The conversation certainly *contains* the Hough–Leavis idea that

matriarchal possessiveness is under attack; Birkin states this quite explicitly:

> 'I don't want to serve you, because there is nothing there to serve. What you want me to serve, is nothing, mere nothing. It isn't even you, it is your mere female quality. And I wouldn't give a straw for your female ego – it's a rag doll.' (XIX.327)

But as in the comparable conversation of Chapter XIII, the narrative records Ursula's resistance as well as Birkin's assertion. Do we feel that Ursula is displaying the domineering oppressiveness of female supremacy; or rather standing up for herself against the insistent demands of one who is more concerned to assert his own egoism, to subdue the woman to his *patriarchal* power, than to achieve a genuinely mutual relation of equality?

> 'You only want your own ends. You don't want to serve *me*, and yet you want me to serve you . . . You are just egocentric . . . You want yourself really, and your own affairs. And you want me just to be there, to serve you . . . You want me to be your thing, never to criticize you or to have anything to say for myself . . .'
> 'I want you not to care about yourself, just to be there and not to care about yourself, not to insist . . .'
> 'Who insists?' she mocked. 'Who is it that keeps on insisting? It isn't *me*'.
> '. . . But he, too, had his idea and his will. (XIX.327–9).

The *dramatic* scene which directly follows the *symbolic* scene thus seems to pose the problem as that of two opposed, conflicting 'wills', Two egos that need to be broken apart – the power of matriarchal dominance and the force of patriarchal bullying.

The 'meanings' of the novel seem here to be definitely located in this kind of overtly 'poetic', symbolic writing; and those meanings point insistently to philosophical and metaphysical levels of thought. 'Moony' is another 'ritual scene' (see above, Chapter Four, pp. 66–7) in which an individual enacts by ritual gestures his/her relationship with the circumambient universe. The conflicts which beset Birkin and Ursula at an emotional and psychological level are thus related to immense universal forces, operating through and around the individual and his relationships. Before writing the novel Lawrence had in fact developed a perspective on human life which disposed him to keep his own, and his reader's attention focused on a larger, 'visionary' universe. Before the outbreak of war in 1914, Lawrence developed as an artist by writing and publishing in the three traditional literary kinds – novel, poetry and drama. In the early years of the war he began to write and publish more non-fictional discursive prose, of a philosophical and metaphysical kind, in which he offered often polemical opinions on matters of ethics, politics, psychology, religion. After *Women in Love* his novels became increasingly dominated by the need to transmit these ideas so that his reputation became in the 1920s that of a prophet and sage as much as a writer or artist. The significance of this development for *Women in Love* is that by the time it was written between 1916 and 1917, Lawrence had become increasingly preoccupied with philosophical speculation and increasingly committed to prophetic expression.

We need at this point to consider some contextual factors which bore upon the shaping of *Women in Love*. When Lawrence submitted to the publishers Methuen in 1914 his novel *The Rainbow* (under the title of *The Wedding Ring*) it was rejected as 'impossible for publication in its present form'. This rejection, combined with the impact of the war, induced Lawrence to begin writing (in September 1914) a critical and philosophical book *The Study of Thomas Hardy*[9]: 'What a miserable world. What colossal idiocy, this war. Out of sheer rage I've begun my book about Thomas Hardy', he wrote to his agent on 5 September 1914[10]. *The Rainbow* was finally published in September 1915, and immediately suppressed as obscene. *Women in Love* was then written in three drafts, April–June 1916, July–October 1916, and May–December 1917. During the same period Lawrence wrote and rewrote *The Study of Thomas Hardy*; another philosophical essay, *The Crown*, designed as his contribution to an intellectual anti-war effort; and a further philosophical treatise *The Reality of Peace*. Throughout the composition of *Women in Love* Lawrence's urge to write philosophical treatises (an impulse sparked off by the war) was a constantly present contextual factor.

In January 1914 Lawrence declared an explicitly religious or metaphysical vision as the new context of his writing:[11]

> The Laocoön writhing and shrieking have gone from my new work, and I think there is a bit of stillness, like the wide, still, unseeing eyes of a Venus of Melos ... There is something in the Greek sculpture that my soul is hungry for – something of the eternal stillness that lies under all movement, under all life, like a source, incorruptible and inexhaustible. It is deeper than change, and struggling. So long I have acknowledged only the struggle, the stream, the change. And now I begin to feel something of the source, the stream, the great impersonal which never changes and out of which all change comes.

If a novelist's attention is directed towards that 'eternal stillness', the 'great impersonal', rather than the mobile flux of struggle and change, the character of his art will be profoundly affected: and he will be less concerned with methods of representing 'movement', more preoccupied with techniques for penetrating through movement to stillness, through the visible flux of reality to the 'great impersonal which never changes'. *The Study of Thomas Hardy* shows that in the novels of the earlier writer Lawrence found just such an awareness of man in relation to some great cosmic background rather than in relation to human society and history:

> Upon the vast, incomprehensible pattern of some primal morality greater than the human mind can grasp, is drawn the little pathetic pattern of man's moral life and struggle, pathetic, almost ridiculous . . . This is the quality Hardy shares with the great writers, Shakespeare or Sophocles or Tolstoi, this setting behind the small action of his protagonists the terrific action of unfathomed nature; setting a smaller system of morality, the one grasped and formulated by the human consciousness, within the vast, uncomprehending and incomprehensible morality of nature or of life itself, surpassing human consciousness.[12]

Human societies (the province of realistic fiction) are reduced in this vision to tiny 'ridiculous' patterns of morality dwarfed by the 'terrific action of unfathomed nature' which surrounds them. The important relationship is not that social bond between human beings which is governed by a human code of morality: but the connection between human individuals and the great impersonal forces of the universe.

> Through studying Hardy's art and Hardy's people, Lawrence had found a language in which to conceive the impersonal forces he saw operating within and between human beings: involving a new clarification of what the novel he had been trying to write was really *about*; and the discovery of a 'structural skeleton' on which to re-found it in a new dimension.[13]

It was in his essay 'The Crown' that Lawrence evolved his theory of the two parallel and simultaneous processes, creation and disintegration which we've already encountered in *Women in Love*:

> Destruction and Creation are the two relative absolutes between the opposing infinities. Life is in both. Life may even, for a while, be almost entirely in one, or almost entirely in the other. For life is really the two, the absolute is the pure relation which is both. If we have our fill of destruction, then we shall turn again to creation.

The existence of such philosophical pronouncements (in these works of discursive prose which represent Lawrence's intervention into the cultural politics of First World War British society), can make a profound difference to the way we read *Women in Love*. In the novel (e.g. XIV.238) we witness a character propounding a philosophy of life, based on the conception of a dialectic of creation and destruction. Birkin may intend his metaphysic of opposed universal principles as purely symbolic rather than actual, or he may be

articulating a profound belief in the *literal* existence of such universal
forces. Either way, the reader is likely to understand the concept as
symbolism or metaphor: the imagery of the two rivers is there to
assist our understanding of the social and psychological forces at
work around and between the novel's personal relations. Clearly
there would be nothing difficult or unusual about this: all novels use
metaphor and symbolism. But what if the novel is actually attempting to persuade us that the world it depicts does literally contain or
exemplify the actions of a force of universal disintegration? Lawrence was certainly seeking in *The Crown* to persuade his readers
that such propositions were *literally* true: and as the act of communication was articulated in the midst of the carnage and destructiveness
of the war, his arguments could have carried great rhetorical force, if
not actual logical weight. Are we meant to take the novel's
philosophical propositions as symbolic or as literally true? At what
point does metaphor shade into myth and metaphysic? In 1915
Lawrence recorded seeing a Zeppelin in the sky over London, in
these terms:[14]

> . . . There was war in heaven . . . It seemed as if the cosmic order were
> gone, as if there had come a new order . . . It seems our cosmos has
> burst, burst at last . . . it is the end, our world has gone . . . But there
> must be a new heaven and a new earth.

Is Lawrence speaking *metaphorically* here – meaning that it *feels* like
the end of the world, that things are changing out of all recognition,
that now is the time to found a new society? Or are such statements
to be read as literal truth?

> When Lawrence spoke of 'signs' he did not mean only that everything
> was getting very bad, he meant there *were* apocalyptic images and
> signs in the sky. The Zeppelin was one . . .[15]

It is true that Lawrence considered various titles for *Women in Love*,
among them *Dies Irae (Day of Wrath)*, and *The Latter Days*, both
referring to the Day of Judgement.[16] Did he intend such suggestions
metaphorically, or did he literally believe that his world was doomed
to some great cosmic cataclysm?

It has been argued[17] that Lawrence was an 'apocalyptic' thinker,
drawing on traditions of mythological primitivism as a way of understanding the events of his time – not as social problem, economic collapse or historical turbulence, but as a universal or cosmic crisis.
Lawrence himself admitted that the biblical *Book of Revelations*,
together with other apocalyptic writings such as nonconformist
hymns, coloured his imagination in childhood; and towards the
end of his life he wrote several essays on *Revelations* and other

apocalyptic themes.[18] During the early years of the war he began to use the language of apocalypse extensively – writing of a universal decadence and a coming resurrection; the end of the world, and the birth of a new heaven and a new earth. From this milennialist heritage Lawrence derived a tendency to see history in terms of cycles, crises and transitions; an obsessive preoccupation with 'the last days' and their anticipated terrors; a conviction that decadence must precede renovation; a belief in the possibility for some perilous salvation for a tiny 'elect'; and a faith that such salvation might be attainable through the practice of certain esoteric mysteries.[19] What difference do such suggestions make to the way in which we read *Women in Love*?

Please read Chapter XIX ('Moony') from p. 330, 'Suddenly he found himself face to face with a situation' to the end of the chapter; and consider the following questions.

1 What significance does the West African statuette (described earlier in the novel, VI.127, VII.123) bear in Birkin's meditations?

2 Does the novel seem to be suggesting that the two routes to racial death which Birkin defines are actual historical processes, literally occurring in the actual world? How closely should we identify Birkin's thoughts with Lawrence's beliefs? Does the language operate to promote or to inhibit the transmission of ideas?

3 How does Birkin define his own beliefs *vis-à-vis* the traditionally positive values of 'goodness, holiness, desire for creation and productive happiness'? (XIX.330)

4 Does Lawrence at this point seem to be forsaking the novel form in favour of mythological and metaphysical speculation?

DISCUSSION

1 The West African statuette was employed earlier in the novel (in the chapter entitled 'Totem') to symbolize a 'pure culture in sensation, culture in the physical consciousness, really ultimate, *physical* consciousness, mindless, utterly sensual' (VII.133). Evidently this emblematic figure functions as a kind of 'totem' for the decadent London Bohemians; Gerald is profoundly impressed by it, and identifies it with the Pussum; and there Birkin acknowledges its importance for him: 'she was one of his soul's intimates' (XIX.330). Here the figure functions as a symbolic basis for Birkin's definition of 'the African way', a process of 'disintegration and dissolution' supposed to have been lived through by an earlier civilization, and now happening again to modern Europe:

There is a long way we can travel, after the death-break; after that
point where the soul in intense suffering breaks, breaks away from its
organic hold like a leaf that falls. We fall from the connection with
life and hope, we lapse from pure, integral being, from creation
and liberty, and we fall into the long, long, African process of purely
sensual understanding, knowledge in the mystery of dissolution.
(XIX.330–1)

2   Birkin's meditations postulate a metaphysical and apocalyptic
theory of history: at a certain historical moment a race 'dies' in a
mystical sense, begins or attains a degree of decadence in which 'the
relation between the senses and the outspoken mind' is ruptured.
What happened to the Africans is being repeated in his own society;
he experiences the process in his own being: 'That which was immi-
nent in himself must have taken place in these Africans' (XIX.330).

   Birkin seeks a different imagery to articulate his vision of the
death of the white races:

It would be done differently by the white races. The white races, having the arctic north behind them, the vast abstraction of ice and snow,
would fulfil a mystery of ice-destructive knowledge, snow-abstract
annihilation . . . Birkin thought of Gerald. He was one of these strange
white wonderful demons from the north, fulfilled in the destructive
frost-mystery. And was he fated to pass away in this knowledge, this
one process of frost-knowledge, death by perfect cold? Was he a mes-
senger, an omen of the universal dissolution into whiteness and
snow?   (XIX.331)

The narrative defines these ideas as 'speculation': are they in fact any
more than the random thoughts of an alienated individual? Isn't the
novel presenting us with an image of a particular man, interested in
primitive art and prone to metaphysical disquisition, giving form to
a body of eccentric and unconvincing doctrines? We have seen in earlier discussions that Birkin's ideas are not necessarily privileged; and
his subsequent attempts in this chapter to implement his metaphysical revelation in practice fall very flat indeed (XIX.333–9).

   Yet, despite these factors, the passage has a compelling centrality and conviction. The lack of any firm distinction between narrative
voice and character-consciousness (see above pp. 5–7) gives Birkin's
speculations a free rein to impose themselves as portentous
metaphysical generalizations, of a type that the author was himself
making simultaneously in his letters. Repetitive and incantatory
techniques in the prose operate to secure maximum persuasiveness
for the rhetoric – consider the repetitive play in one paragraph with the
words 'knowledge', 'senses' and 'dissolution' (XIX.330). Most significant of all is the fact that Birkin's vision of the death of Gerald is

genuinely prophetic: in the novel's close Gerald does indeed perish by 'dissolution into whiteness and snow' (XIX.331; see XXX.573–5). That individual death prompts Birkin once again to reflections on the deaths of races and civilizations: (XXX.580) the prophetic accuracy of his forebodings and the persuasive rhetoric of his speculations operate to confirm Gerald as an adequate representative of the 'white races', and to ratify the mythical and metaphysical level of discourse.
3   There appears to be no possibility of avoiding this break with 'integral being, creation and liberty': the only choice is whether one seeks 'knowledge in dissolution and corruption' – a perverse sensuality that savours and luxuriates in the flux of corruption – or attempts to discover another way out. This is Birkin's 'way of freedom':

> There was another way, the way of freedom. There was the paradisal entry into pure, single being, the individual soul taking precedence over love and desire for union, stronger than any pangs of emotion, a lovely state of free-proud singleness . . .   (XIX.332).

This apparently decisive revelation is actually the most difficult and ambiguous part of the passage. Birkin's 'way of freedom' is often identified (by Leavis, for example – see above p. 44) with those traditional positive values named as 'goodness, holiness, desire for creation and productive happiness'. Lawrence himself, in a letter of November 1915 employed a language and a conceptual framework similar to the passage from *Women in Love*: a faith in 'integral unity' and 'the spirit of love and creation' is opposed to the 'disintegrating process' of war.[20] Such a language can be sustained only by a continuing belief in communal values and co-operative effort: but, as we will see in the next chapter, Lawrence's experience of the war gradually forced him back into an extremity of isolation and an acute alienation, until he could see individual fulfilment and happiness as possibly only in an escape from society, even from history:

> The only thing to be done now is either to go down with the ship, or as much as one can, leave the ship, and like a castaway live a life apart. As for me, I do not belong to the ship; I will not, if I can help it, sink with it. I reject it. As far as I possibly can I will stand outside this time, I will live my life, and if possible be happy, while the whole world slides in horror down into the bottomless pit.   (February, 1916)[21]

Birkin's concept of happiness relates only to himself and Ursula: there is no point at which the relationship can feed back into the world of society. 'Goodness, holiness, desire for creation and productive happiness' are renounced by Birkin as completely as by the sensual Africans or the demons of the arctic north. Indeed, it would

be a matter of some surprise if this novel were found to be promulga-
ting such traditional liberal virtues: Lawrence himself described it as
'purely destructive'.[22]

4   Though the metaphysical or apocalyptic may be the characteristic mode of Lawrence's imagination, he remains a novelist: and as a
novelist he retains a firm grasp on the actuality of human behaviour
which acts to keep the metaphysical in check. The product of Birkin's
esoteric self-communing is a very familiar fictional decision – a proposal of marriage.[23] We might add that the proposal, as it is narrated
later in the chapter (XIX.332–40) is a debacle: the issue may be
resolved on the metaphysical level, but it remains to be successfully executed in practice. Frank Kermode finds throughout *Women
in Love* a continuous creative dialectic between the universali-
zing abstraction of metaphysic and the concrete historicizing
of fiction:

> Does a new world – created in the burning out of sexual shame, in the
> birth from such an icy womb as that of the last chapters of Lawrence's
> novel – does such a world await the elect when the terrors of the trans-
> ition are over? Do the elect rightly look forward to the epoch of the
> Holy Spirit? The myth in the book says yes . . . the novel fights back at
> myth, and where the myth says yes, the novel and Ursula often say no.
> The novel, as a kind, belongs to humanism, not to mystery religion
> . . . it cannot, because of the society that produced it, abandon
> empathy entirely in favour of abstraction.[24]

Please read *Women in Love* Chapter XXIII ('Excurse') and consider
the following questions.

1   Look up the word 'Excurse' in a dictionary. Did it mean what you
     thought it did?
2   The chapter falls technically into two distinct halves: a fairly
     realistic account of a drive, a quarrel and a reconciliation; and an
     overtly symbolic, even 'metaphysical' account of the spiritual
     'marriage' of Ursula and Birkin. Are the two halves completely
     distinct, or interpenetrating?
3   How do you respond to the kind of language Lawrence begins to
     use, from 'unconsciously, with her sensitive finger-tips'
     (XXIII.395) to the end of the chapter? Do you think the language
     conveys with adequate definition the significance of the lovers'
     union? Does it distinguish the quality of their physical experience
     from the 'African way' of dark sensuality Birkin has previously
     rejected? Does it distinguish their union clearly from that of
     Gerald and Gudrun?

DISCUSSION

1 Most people read the word as 'excursion', and as the chapter is
about Birkin and Ursula taking a trip in a car, that seems entirely
appropriate. In fact is is a verb whose primary sense is that of 'to
wander, digress' from some expected direction or familiar norm;
though it has a secondary sense, to 'go on an excursion'. The arousal
of different meanings seems deliberate:

> 'Where are we? she asked suddenly.
> 'Not far from Worksop'.
> 'And where are we going?'
> 'Anywhere'.   (XXIII.385)

An excursion through a familiar landscape becomes a mysterious,
unpredictable voyage into undiscovered countries. Several chapter
titles in the later part of the novel; 'Threshold', 'Flitting', 'Exeunt' –
repeat this emphasis on departure, transition, the bidding farewell to
one world and the exploration of another.

2 The chapter certainly moves decisively from realistic presentation to metaphysical discovery:

> The car was runing along a broad white road, between autumn
> trees.   (XXIII.383)

> With perfect fine finger-tips of reality she would touch the reality in
> him, the suave, pure, untranslatable reality of his loins of darkness.
> (XXIII.402)

> She knew that, in accepting the rings, she was accepting a pledge.
> (XXIII.385).

> She recalled again the old magic of the Book of Genesis, where the
> sons of God saw the daughters of men, that they were fair. And he was
> one of those, one of those strange creatures from the beyond, looking
> down at her, and seeing that she was fair.   (XXIII.395)

The account of the drive, the gift of the rings, the quarrel, is all presented realistically. Yet as he drives the car Birkin's meditations are
anything but the everyday reflections of the conscious mind:

> He had taken her at the roots of her darkness and shame – like a
> demon, laughing over the fountain of mystic corruption . . .
> (XXIII.386).

And while the lovers are encountering one another on a new plane of
mystic 'reality', the narrative constantly acknowledges the pressures
and claims of a more ordinary conception of the real: the inn, the

tea-room, the meal; the resignations, and Birkin's concern about scandal; the telegram to Ursula's father; the 'bread, and cheese, and raisins, and apples, and hard chocolate' that Birkin purchases from a shop. Earlier critics found this constant interconnecting of the metaphysical and the mundane ridiculous. Middleton Murry laughed at the transition from 'the deepest life-force' to an *à la carte* menu:[25]

> ... 'the deepest physical mind' has no sense of humour. Why, in the name of darkness, 'a venison pasty, *of all things*' (XXIII.397)? Is a venison pasty more incongruous with this beatitude than a large ham?

And many other readers have been equally unimpressed by Lawrence's attempts to unify the mythical and the modern: 'He sat still like an Egyptian Pharoah, driving the car', (XXIII.400). Some critics however argue that Lawrence's persistence in anchoring the metaphysical to the concrete particulars of material living is evidence that he remained aware of his responsibilities as a novelist: the need to remind the reader 'that this is life', the need to insist on the unity of spirit and flesh, essence and existence, myth and history.

> The chapter called 'Excurse' illustrates most of the risks and achievements. Here is the climactic struggle – starting in a new-fangled car at the side of the road. Ursula accuses Birkin of deathly obscenity ... They are interrupted by a passing bicyclist ... That bicyclist is very typical of Lawrence. But the hardest part is to come: the love-scene in the Saracen's Head, her fingers tracing the life-flow in his thighs. At last she is a daughter of man with one of the sons of God. From somewhere 'deeper than the phallic source' she gets the necessary knowledge of what lies beyond love and passion. They eat a large meal, plan the future, drive off ...
>
> It is in such passages that Lawrence dares the reader to take the profound for the ridiculous; the bicyclist, the meal, the telegram, are all there to remind one that this is life, not a scribble to be resolved by reference to some doctrine, not a fantasy either. (Frank Kermode, 1973)[26]

3   The scene is a love-scene, and one of the discourses it employs is a familiar 'romantic' language of transfiguring love:

> It was as if she were enchanted, and everything were metamorphosed ... her face that was upturned exactly like a flower ... a paradisal flower she was, beyond womanhood. (XXIII.395–6)

This 'romantic' language is pushed further in the direction of transcendence to suggest that the union is a mystical experience, beyond ordinary human comprehension:

> Quenched, inhuman, his fingers upon her unrevealed nudity were the fingers of silence upon silence, the body of mysterious night upon the

> body of mysterious night, the night masculine and femine, never to be seen with the eye, or known with the mind, only known as a palpable revelation of mystic otherness. (XXIII.403)

It is the manner in which this 'mystic' perception is articulated that presents readers with the greatest difficulty. The more conventionally 'romantic' language focuses on the face, emphasizing brightness and an upward and outward motion, as in the recurrent image of the flower. Much of the language employed here expresses on the contrary a *downward* rhythm, and emphasizes the lower parts of the body:

> ... she was tracing the backs of his thighs, following some mysterious life-flow there. She had discovered something, something more than wonderful, more wonderful than life itself. It was the strange mystery of his life-motion, there, at the back of the thighs, down the flanks ... behold, from the smitten rock of the man's body, from the strange marvellous flanks and thighs, deeper, further in mystery than the phallic source, came the floods of ineffable darkness and ineffable riches. (XXII.395,397)

If this language is assimilated to the novel's metaphysical dialectic of creativity and disintegration, it brings us closer to the 'dark river of dissolution' than to the 'silver river of life': a mystical lovers' union involves an appreciation of those 'floods of ineffable darkness' that flow from the base ('smitten rock') of the man's body, and relate linguistically to the 'flux of corruption'.[27] Colin Clarke sees this feature as characteristic of the novel's insistence that new life can be generated only in the process of reduction:

> Commentators have written-off this episode with monotonous unanimity ... what has disturbed some critics is the similarity of certain phrases to the phrasing in that passage about the African fetish, in 'Moony': we cannot but compare 'deeper than the phallic source', 'deeper, further in mystery than the phallic source' (XXIII.397) with 'How far, in their inverted culture, had these West Africans gone beyond phallic knowledge?, (XIX.331) and 'this was far beyond any phallic knowledge, sensual subtle realities far beyond the scope of phallic investigation'. This oblique analogy, in the opinion of the critics in question, is evidence of a spiritual sickness in Birkin and Ursula (who yet, they claim, is clearly meant to embody a norm) and evidence therefore of a failure in artistic control. Yet the passage in 'Excurse' positively *invites* comparison with the earlier one, as it also does, for that matter, with that passage in 'Water-Party' about the river of dissolution ... At the very moment when the lovers release in themselves a full flow of life we are encouraged to note the analogy with the flux of corruption, and even, indeed, with the awful African process ... life is affirmed in reduction ... it is only another instance of that positive reductive process of dissolution to which the novel as a whole is one comprehensive tribute.[28]

Leavis found the language of this chapter verging on 'jargon', and evidence of a radical uncertainty about what Lawrence wanted to say.[29] Colin Clarke suggests reasons for the resistance to this language of critics such as Leavis, who are bent on clarifying a formal 'symmetry of negative and positive' in the novel's moral design: far from articulating a clear *alternative* to the various available routes to degeneration and dissolution (a linguistic equivalent of Birkin's 'way of freedom'), Clarke suggests that the prose recalls Birkin's own definition of 'the African way' of acquiring mystic knowledge from the process of disintegration. The moralistic attempt to distinguish creative and positive from destructive and negative tendencies founders on the obstacle of this complex prose, which insistently confuses creative and destructive principles.

Earlier in the chapter, Ursula launches a blistering attack on Birkin (XXIII.387–90) for being 'deathly', 'obscene', 'foul and perverse', which probably seems like a blow for moral health; it certainly provokes Birkin to a self-criticism:

> He knew that his spirituality was concomitant of a process of depravity, a sort of pleasure in self-destruction.   (XXIII.391)

He doesn't, however, promise to renounce it – 'He knew it, and had done' (XXIII.391). At that point Birkin's physical/spiritual desire for Ursula is articulated in a language of 'darkness', 'shame', 'corruption', and 'death' (XXIII.386); far from superseding this decadent prose, with its covert though obvious references to anal sex, the later union of Birkin and Ursula confirms it.

Let us finally consider whether this passage confirms or confutes the attempts we've already considered to separate and distinguish the love-relationships of Birkin/Ursula and Gerald/Gudrun. Compare these passages from 'Excurse' with the language describing Gudrun's emotions, at *Women in Love*, Chapter XIV, pp. 248–9:

> She seemed to faint, beneath, and he seemed to faint, stooping over her. It was a perfect passing away for both of them, and at the same time the most intolerable accession into being . . . the sense of the awfulness of riches that could never be impaired flooded her mind like a swoon, a death in most marvellous possession, mystic-sure. She possessed him so utterly and intolerably, that she herself lapsed out. (XXIII.396, 399).

Or compare this with *Women in Love*, Chapter IX ('Coal-Dust'), pp. 174–5:

> She traced with her hands the line of his loins and thighs, at the back, and a living fire ran through her, from him, darkly. It was a dark flood of electric passion she released from him, drew into herself. She had

established a rich new circuit, a new current of passional electric
energy, between the two of them, released from the darkest poles of
the body and established in perfect circuit. (XXIII.396)

The first passage contains the same emphasis on fainting, passing
away, swooning, death, lapsing out – with the repetition of 'intolerable', as the earlier passage describing Gudrun's feelings when confronted with Gerald's 'loins'. The second passage employs recurrent
imagery of electricity – 'electric passion', 'circuit', 'poles' – thus
recalling the 'intolerable deep resonance' of mechanized Beldover
which so fascinates Gudrun. What possibilities are there for drawing
an absolute moral distinction between experiences that are articulated in almost identical language?

Critics who acknowledge these difficulties – such as Ford,
Clarke and Kinkead-Weekes – tend to reconcile them by adopting
roughly the same argument, which they derive from Lawrence's
philosophical treatises. This involves the proposition that Lawrence
was acutely aware of the interdependence and interpenetration of
'creation' and 'dissolution', the two opposed, 'rivers of life'; but that
he still wanted to make a comprehensive moral distinction on the
basis of that antithesis. It was impossible, Lawrence held, to remain
aloof from the river of dissolution; yet it should be possible to ebb
with the dark stream in order to reach the current of new life which
is its counterpart and opposite. Birkin, it is argued, does this: while
other characters either attempt to deny or stem the negative tide
(such as Gerald's father, and partly Gerald himself); while others,
such as Gudrun and Loerke, immerse themselves in it to obtain a perverse and decadent gratification from the experience of corruption
and putrescence (see XVII.285–6, and below pp. 117–19; and
XXIX, 522–3). I myself find it more difficult to disentangle positive
from negative, integral being from disintegration, creativity from
dissolution, in a complex fictional medium which seems determined
to connect, even validate, both. The reasons for Lawrence's interfus-
ing of moral and metaphysical opposites seems to me connected with
his apocalyptic perspective, in turn determined by his own relation as
a writer to the society of his time, the Britain of 1914–20: the Britain
of the First World War.

6. Biography, History

Women in Love XVII, XXVI, XXIX

A question I haven't raised in discussing these metaphysical and apocalyptic versions of the novel – but which you might well have asked yourself – is this: what precise status and value do we attach to such ideas, given that the novel itself accords them considerable weight and seriousness, and that the novelist himself seems to have actually (in some degree) believed them? Do we simply ignore the beliefs embodied in a novel, receiving some aesthetic or imaginative impression independent of ideas? Or is our appreciation of the novel to some extent conditional on our acceptance of the attitudes it appears to express? Literary criticism often fails to face up to this problem. A critic such as Frank Kermode, whose work was addressed in the previous chapter, can handle the most bizarre and esoteric ideas with great *savoir-faire*, because they are to him aesthetic objects, which offer themselves for the inspection of his curiosity rather than impose on him with the challenge of belief. His enormous familiarity with cultural history shows him how human societies have lived by so many different belief-systems that it would be impossible to interpret all works of art from a position of acquiescence in their ideas. The obvious answer is to adopt the perspective which in philosophy is called relativism: an avoidance of value-judgements and a promiscuous, epicurean delighting in all artefacts and all opinions.

The problem with such an approach is its neglect of history: ideas come to possess a logic and a life of their own, and are always explained in relation to other ideas. Once literary criticism has succeeded in breaking away from the constraints of mimetic and representational concepts of fiction, it becomes vulnerable to the danger of attributing to cultural productions a false autonomy and independence of historical determination, social function and ideological character. The 'New Criticism' of the 1950s (which based its methods primarily in poetry rather than the novel) often fell into this trap: if literature doesn't imitate the 'real' world, then it must be either purely autonomous ('art for art's sake') or imitative of some transcendental ideal. Much 'post-structuralist' literary criticism seems to me to court the same peril – the denial of history – with often damaging effect.

It is possible in literary criticism and theory to take works of fiction on their own terms – to acknowledge their uniqueness of design and their relative autonomy, not to judge them as good or bad copies of something else – without denying that they have their origins in a real historical situation, and inevitably have some kind of complex and mediated relationship with the 'real' of history. If we feel that there is something sterile and pointless in explaining fiction by reference to ideas, we will perhaps be more interested in tracing the source and the referent, of both ideas and art, to the author's living relationship with historical place and time.

We have seen that the novel to some degree endorses the extremism of apocalyptic ideas. But now consider a scene which might dispose you to reflect rather differently on the book's metaphysical finality. Please read Chapter XXIII, pp. 397–9, from 'Everything is ours' to 'It's you and me, isn't it?' What do you make of Birkin's statements, and to what extent is Ursula in sympathy with them?

DISCUSSION

The achievement of successful relationship, the reconciliation of conflict in mutuality, produces an immediate decision: the two lovers resign from their jobs and resolve to leave England. Where they intend to go and what they intend to do remains undefined and still, at the end of the novel, unresolved. The sudden resolution to 'get out, quick' (XXIII.397) seems precipitated by the attainment of a 'perfected relation' (398) between Ursula and Birkin; though in fact the escapist impulse has been present throughout the novel. Their 'perfected relation' provides them in fact with the basis they need to execute their profoundest desire – to contract out of society, and embark on a voyage without destination.

The passage is a typically complex confrontation of different views. Birkin is, as usual, adamant and dogmatic: Ursula seems in agreement, but she is far more hesitant and tentative – 'wondering', 'doubtfully', 'quizzically'. She greets Birkin's proposals that they should 'wander' to 'nowhere' with scepticism: 'wandering seemed to her like restlessness, dissatisfaction'; 'But to her it was only travel' (XXIII.398). Where Birkin affirms his belief in the possibility of entry to an alternative world – 'One wants to wander away from the world's somewheres, into our own nowhere' (398) – Ursula insists that there is no such escape: 'we've got to take the world that's given – because there isn't any other' (398). Where Birkin envisages some isolated *émigré* community living in freedom and tranquility, Ursula prefers the traditional otherworld of perfect love. The passage draws attention to the vagueness of Birkin's ideas, and the sceptical dissatisfaction of Ursula's responses: it deliberately refuses to confirm any effect of resolution, harmony, completeness.

We might find this odd in itself, in the writing of an apocalyptic and metaphysical thinker: the ancient clarities of mythical design are complicated by a typically modern emphasis on the uncertain, the unfinished, the inconclusive. It is perhaps even odder when we consider that Lawrence was handling here material of a partially autobiographical nature. In his letters we can find the author asserting exactly such a desire to be liberated from the process of history: 'I will not live any more in this time . . . I reject it . . . I will stand outside this time.'[1] The letter is an affirmation which Lawrence tried to live through. The novel subjects the same affirmation to interrogation, casting over it the illumination of an inquisitive scepticism. Let us look at some facts of Lawrence's life in order to understand how he reached the apocalyptic position, which he then found it necessary to renounce.

He was born in 1885 in Eastwood, a mining village in the East Midlands coalfield. His father was a miner, his mother a former schoolteacher. His childhood was dominated by a possessive mother-love and by the personal and social conflicts bitterly fought out between mother and father: these experiences he transformed into fiction in *Sons and Lovers* (1913). He was educated at a local Board School and won a County Council Scholarship to Nottingham High School. Leaving in 1901, he worked as a clerk in a surgical appliances factory until a severe attack of pnemonia forced a termination of his employment. In 1902 he became a pupil-teacher at the British School, Eastwood, and from there qualified himself to take a two-year teacher's certificate course at Nottingham University College. Between this period and 1908 he began writing prose and

D. H. Lawrence's birthplace, Eastwood
'The houses with slate roofs and blackish brick walls . . .'
Women in Love, IX.173

Higher Tregerthen Farm, Zennor, Cornwall
'there's somewhere where we can be free . . .'
Women in Love, XXIII.398

short stories, and his first novel, which became *The White Peacock* (1911). Between 1908 and 1911 he taught at a school in Croydon, and began to come to the attention of London literary figures such as Edward Marsh. His second novel, *The Trespasser* (1912) was written here. It was also in 1912 that he met Frieda Weekley, German wife of his former tutor at Nottingham, and the daughter of the Baron von Richthofen. Six weeks later he eloped with her to Germany. Settling in Italy he finished *Sons and Lovers* and began to write *The Sisters*, the novel which was later split into *The Rainbow* and *Women in Love*.

Prior to the onset of war Lawrence seemed well established in the beginnings of a successful literary career. He was noticed by prominent writers and cultural entrepreneurs, his work was being published, he was in sympathy with some contemporary literary developments (such as 'Georgian' poetry).[2] The general cultural situation in Britain was healthy and progressive, a widespread liberal reaction against the Victorian orthodoxies of the previous generation. More avant-garde writing of the kind Lawrence was soon to produce was still very much the work of cultural exiles, for whom the centre was Paris; it would probably be a mistake to assume that Edwardian England, even without the war, was quite ready for *The Rainbow*; any more than it was ready for *Ulysses*. But it was the war that isolated Lawrence and obstructed his progress as a public writer. The literary intelligentsia split, with many prominent writers being enlisted for ideological service,[3] and others forming a pacifistic oppositional group centred on Cambridge, Bloomsbury and Garsington, the home of Lady Ottoline Morrell.[4] Lawrence's working-class origins rendered his relations with both Bloomsbury literati and Cambridge intellectuals extremely difficult: as his sympathies were neither pacifist, liberal nor democratic, he found it impossible to sustain any accord with, for example, Bertrand Russell's rationalist and democratic programmes for social reconstruction.[5] Lawrence's isolation and his sense of being alienated within British society were finally compounded by the suppression of *The Rainbow*; a critical event over which he believed the intelligentsia, by its failure to defend the novel, had betrayed him.

Above all, perhaps Lawrence was isolated by the visionary extremism of his opinions. Before the war he had been developing a critique of modern industrial civilization, which he regarded as a corrupt, sterile and inhuman social form.[6] He believed that the war was a product of that society, and had no patience with any oppositional tendency that didn't reject the industrial system outright. Hence his dismissal of socialist movements and ideas, which seemed to him merely a mechanical reaction, the counterpart not the opposite of industrial capitalism. His own hostility to industrialism was based on the Romantic–humanist tradition of social criticism,[7] and it was from that legacy that he sought to draw an oppositional ethic. Thus his opposition to the war alternated between negotiating schemes for an anti-war political party, and fashioning dreams of establishing an ideal community on a distant foreign shore. The introduction of conscription in 1915 subjected Lawrence to a series of medical examinations for exemption, which he found intensely humiliating and emotionally shocking. The war prevented him from leaving England, as he wished, for America. In 1916 he settled in Cornwall, where he wrote *Women in Love*.

The novel was written out of the most painful and desperate crisis of Lawrence's life. During the early years of the war, both his subjective experience and his personal and social relations became fraught, embittered, full of conflict; and his mental state verged at times on paranoia and profound misanthropy, of which many of Birkin's utterances seem to be the echo:

> My eyes can see nothing human that is good, nowadays: at any rate, nothing public. London seems to be like some hoary massive underworld, a hoary, ponderous inferno. The traffic flows through the rigid grey streets like the rivers of Hell through their banks of dry, rocky ash.[8]

> Yesterday, at Worthing, there were many soldiers. Can I ever tell you how ugly they were . . . it is obscene. I like men to be beasts, but insects . . . they remind me of lice or bugs . . . What massive creeping hell is let loose nowadays.[9]

Though he had hated the war from the very beginning, he could not free himself of it: self-evidently unfit for military service, he was still subjected to bullying and intimidation by state authorities. Serious attempts to participate in some kind of political or intellectual opposition foundered as he failed to secure agreement for his ideas from his collaborators; a prolonged personal disillusionment led him to the desire to escape from his own country and society altogether. While still hopeful of achieving some meaningful intervention, and still committed to co-operative action with others, Lawrence developed a theory of social revolution:[10]

> Now either we have got to break the shell, the frame, the whole form, or we have got to turn to this inward activity of setting the house in order and drawing up a list before we die.
>   But we shall smash the frame. The land, the industries, the means of

communication and the public amusements shall all be nationalized
. . . Then, and only then, shall we be able to begin living. Then we shall
be able to work. Then we can examine love and marriage and all. Till
then, we are fast within the hard, unliving, impervious shell. (1915)

This ambition of transforming a whole society into a living community by revolutionary action then became contracted to the Utopian
longing to escape with a small élite, dedicated to building a new community, based on new social values, in Florida. Lawrence believed
that his plans for Florida were nearing fulfilment (though in fact he
would not have been permitted to leave England) when news came of
the suppression of *The Rainbow*. He was, he said, 'held back to fight'
for his novel by mobilizing influential cultural contacts and literary
acquaintances: to no avail. In Cornwall in 1915 he lived an illusion
of escape, though in fact he was to remain touched and compelled by
the war: suspected of being a foreign agent (with a beard *and* a German wife), forced to undergo further medical examinations, perse-
cuted by the police. Most important of all, with the suppression of
The Rainbow he lost his access to his readership, so that all concrete
sense of an audience fell away from him. He no longer knew for
whom or to whom he was writing: 'One goes on writing, to the
unseen witnesses'.[11]

> Lawrence's life at this time was a constant battleground of social con-
> tradictions. He had been displaced as a miner's son to become a
> respectable professional, displaced from that to become a writer, and
> then displaced by the war from the role of writer itself. He was a writer
> without a public, without access to publication, a man escaping from
> the war and finding that the war relentlessly pursued him. In the midst
> of all this he wrote a novel: 'One must forget, only forget, turn one's
> eyes from the world . . . having another world, as yet uncreated'.

In November 1919 the Lawrences left England for Italy. Thereafter,
Lawrence travelled to, stayed in and wrote about Italy, Sicily,
Ceylon, Australia, New Mexico, Mexico, Switzerland, Mallorca,
and Germany. He died in 1930 at Vence, in the South of France, and
his ashes were interred in New Mexico. After 1919 he had visited
England only twice, in 1923–4 and in 1926.

In a 'Foreword' to *Women in Love*, Lawrence suggested that the
reader should be aware of some relationship between the novel and
the war:

> Written in its first form in the Tyrol, in 1913 . . . altogether rewritten
> and finished in Cornwall in 1917. So that it is a novel which took its
> shape in the midst of the period of war, though it does not concern the
> war itself. I should wish the time to remain unfixed, so that the bitter-
> ness of the war may be taken for granted in the characters.[12]

Think about this passage, and consider these questions:

1   Would it have occurred to you, without knowing the dates of
    writing and without Lawrence's own encouragement, to think of
    Women in Love as a novel which 'took shape in the midst of the
    period of war'?
2   Can you find any evidence of 'the bitterness of the war' in the
    characters?

DISCUSSION

1   In the novel itself chronology seems not to be 'unfixed', but
arrested: since it betrays no indication of the existence of the war
which surrounded and impinged on its making. The world of
Women in Love does appear to be that of pre-1914 England: Gerald,
Birkin says, (VI.116) 'was in the last war', which must (by internal
dating from *The Rainbow*, see Chapter XI) indicate the Boer War of
1899–1902. The characters in the novel are able to take an unevent-
ful railway journey across territory which in 1916 was the battle-
ground and slaughterhouse of Europe.

   The most obvious explanation is to assume that the novel's setting is pre-war, or even that its character was formed before the
experience of war began to colour Lawrence's imagination:

> The life dealt with in *The Rainbow* and *Women in Love* and the
> momentum carrying those works through belong to before the war.
> The spirit of *Women in Love* belongs to a phase when the Bottomley
> horror, the nightmare hopelessness of the later years through which
> the war dragged on, had not yet closed down on Lawrence.[13]

Even if this were proven (and Leavis seems to be ignoring Lawrence's
reference to a complete re-writing in 1917) it still wouldn't answer or
explain the author's own assertion that the war should somehow be
'taken for granted' in the novel.

   Clearly there is no direct link between novel and war: the war is
not immediately present as an experience or a context. There is a
great deal of violence, cruelty, and death in the novel, but it is the violence of personal relationships (VIII, XX), the cruelty of individuals
to their fellow-creatures (IX, XVIII), and the deaths are all in one
doomed family (II, XIV, XVII, XXX). This emphasis could perhaps
be a consequence of a time of great violence and destructiveness, but
equally it could derive from other sources: Lawrence's novel *Sons
and Lovers* (1913) is no less violent, but the causes are class-conflict
and domestic battles rather than war.

We could talk about the alienated condition of the characters, especially Birkin, with more confidence: the odd, quirky, misanthropic, even paranoid condition of Birkin's personality may seem strange in the context of liberal Edwardian England; but is easily intelligible as a response to the war. Lawrence himself, as we have seen, experienced such emotions and developed such an alienated perspective. We can better understand such virulent hatred of society as a response to the conditions of 1914–16.

Finally there is the apocalyptic quality of the novel, which makes more sense when perceived as a way of understanding the war. A feeling of impending calamity, of a doomed civilization drawing to its close, had been strong in British culture from the 1890s onwards; and we have no difficulty now in seeing the unprecedented and universalized modern violence of 1914–18 as the decisive break between the last century and our own. A writer who saw 1914 as the end of an era can command more serious attention than the sandwich-board carrier who exhorts us to repent, for the end is at hand.

These points do not exhaust the possibilities, and they certainly don't solve the problem. How can *Women in Love* be a novel of war if the war is excluded from it?

> Criticism has generally taken the hint offered here, and recognized the war as some kind of context for the novel. But Lawrence's suggestions are contradictory, and in an illuminating way. The novel 'does not concern the war': war does not constitute its subject, and is not the object of its discourse. But the 'bitterness of the war' is to be 'taken for granted' in the characters – so the war, though neither subject nor object, is still somehow inside the novel. If the war is both absent and present in the text, then Lawrence's definition of the time as 'unfixed' presents more than a merely chronological problem.[14]

This quotation suggests that we need to consider other methodological possibilities than that of discovering distant echoes of the war within the novel itself. Think about the following extract from H. M. Daleski's book *The Forked Flame* (1965), and see what you think of it as an attempt at explaining this problem. What is his view of the relationship between novel and war, and do you find it satisfactory?

> Though it is set in the same pre-war England as that in which Ursula of *The Rainbow* reaches maturity, the optimism which, in that book, informs her concluding vision of social regeneration, is transmuted into an abiding sense of the imminent collapse into calamity of a whole way of life. The war, as the viciousness of the fighting bit home by 1916, represented for Lawrence the disintegration of English civilization; and though the novel is apparently remote from the international concerns which agitated men at the time of its composition, it

is, from one point of view, a novel of war, in that it explores the nature
of the deep-seated disease in the body politic of which war is the ultimate death-agony. It is almost as if Lawrence carried out an autopsy
on the still-breathing form of pre-war society.[15]

Daleski attempts a more subtle explanation which acknowledges the
co-existence of novel and war, without trying to separate them in
time and space. The war is seen as the 'ultimate death-agony' of modern industrial society, and the product of a 'deep-seated disease', the
symptoms of which were observable at an earlier stage of that society's development. As a historical generalization this is very convincing: clearly one could write a historical novel about the early seven-
teenth century, disclosing and exploring the historical contradictions
that were later to break forth as the English Civil War. As literary
criticism it is less satisfactory, since it enables the critic to defer the
war to an anticipated cataclysm, and so to exclude the war from the
novel as the novel itself does. The society the novel addresses remains
a complete, though diseased, organic body, yet to reach the terminal
stages of its illness; the novel itself is permitted an organic wholeness
unruptured by the contradiction between Lawrence's immediate
experience and his distancing imagination.

I will take up this theoretical point again at the end of the chapter. Meanwhile, let us think about what's valuable in Daleski's argument: his recognition of the relationship between war and modern
industrial society. Though the novel doesn't mention the war, it is
consistently preoccupied with industrialism and industrial society.
We have already considered in this context the novel's presentation
of the mining town of Beldover (above, Chapter Three, pp. 54–6),
Gerald as a representative of the dominant class of industrial
capitalism (above, Chapter Three, pp. 44–5), the conversation
between Gerald and Birkin in Chapter V ('In the Train') about the
emptiness and sterility of industrial civilization, and so on. The
novel also has a central chapter devoted entirely to an exploration of this theme: Chapter XVII, 'The Industrial Magnate'. Let
us take Daleski's hint and look there for the links between novel
and war.

Please read Chapter XVII of *Women in Love* ('The Industrial
Magnate). Consider the following questions.

1   Summarize the historical process Lawrence postulates in the min-
    ing industry. Does it sound like what Leavis defined as 'essential
    English history'?[16]
2   Can you think of any way in which the social developments
    Lawrence here dramatizes can be related to the war?

DISCUSSION

1   The process of development Lawrence attributes to the mining industry during the 'unfixed' period of the novel has three stages: an initial stage of *laissez-faire* enterprise (Marx's 'primary accumulation') in which both capitalist and worker are enriched, though unequally; a 'paternalistic' stage in which the entrepreneur becomes a philanthropist and uses the 'fortune' he has accumulated from exploiting the workers to deflect and minimize exploitation's damaging effects; and lastly the stage dominated by Gerald, in which the Victorian paternalistic and philanthropic firm is transformed into a modern mechanized system, where the productive mechanism subordinates all human considerations to its own ruthless logic. This process of development is not located exclusively in the mining industry, but is offered as a vision of modern industrial society's development and perfection: a political analysis mounted from an obviously right-wing stance. Beyond this, critics disagree about the precise status and validity of Lawrence's historical generalizations. Leavis, for example, talks guardedly about 'essential' history, suggesting perhaps that this is not so much a verifiably factual history as an interpretation of society's deep spiritual directions:

> His father's dilemma is resolved; and as Gerald goes ahead with his 'life-work' . . . we see in the good-humoured common sense . . . a ruthless inhuman force, and a terrifying reality of the modern world. In some moods, the account of the process may very well strike us as something like the essential human history of the decades since *Women in Love* was written.[16]

John Worthen openly admits that Lawrence's history cannot be considered empirically accurate, but is rather a mythological historiography, analysing and describing a purely autonomous imagined world:

> And it is furthermore generally assumed that 'The Industrial Magnate' is a truly historical account of change . . . critics do not appear to consider that the history of England outlined in 'The Industrial Magnate' is unlike any history they could have read elsewhere . . . The chapter is, in fact, more concerned with myth than with history.[17]

David Craig brings Lawrence's fiction before the bar of actual history, and argues that he underestimated the degree of working-class poverty in the 1890s by extrapolating from his own relatively comfortable working-class childhood, and was thereby able to condemn as 'cupidity' (XVII.298) what was in reality a fight for survival. Lawrence also, in Craig's view, misunderstood the significance of the labour movement: so his 'history' is faulty and misleading in terms of empirical fact and political interpretation:

The sequence is one of the most telling tests of whether Lawrence achieves what Leavis claims for the novel, that it is a 'presentation of twentieth-century England – of modern civilization – so first-hand and searching in its comprehensiveness as to be beyond the powers of any other novelist he knows of'. Presumably such comprehensiveness can't be verified solely by intuition. Doesn't such a claim entail that the work be largely true to what is known to have been the case in the relevant particular situations? . . . it offers an opinion on how things were going for the industrial workers – the majority of English people – which on the face of it is not to me convincing.[18]

As you can see, there is considerable disagreement about the status of this chapter as 'history': from Leavis who thought we should take our history from such writings as *Women in Love*, to David Craig who compares Lawrence's vision unfavourably with the findings of historiography. We could conclude either by condemning the novel as poor historiography, or rescuing it (as John Worthen does) from any responsibility to history, declaring it an autonomous poetic unity.

2   Let's consider whether in fact this peculiar fusion of 'myth' and 'history' cannot be better explained by reference to the war than to the labour struggles of the 1890s. Look at another passage from Daleski:

> Lawrence's criticism of pre-war England is centred in this devastating analysis of Gerald's efficiency. It is one of the points on which the whole novel converges, for if Shortlands meets Beldover in the mines, the miners in turn are clearly a symbol of the industrial complex which is modern civilization and supports alike Breadalby and the Café Pompadour. It is not surprising, therefore, that the word 'disin-tegration' recurs in this passage, though it points to a kind of collapse which, in the nature of the renunciation it epitomizes, is more shock-ing than any yet referred to. This disintegration goes further than the dissolution into separate parts of a whole; the 'reduction' of the miners to 'mere mechanical instruments' is a metamorphosis, the perversity of which is suggested by the name given to the new machines – 'great iron men'. The iron men mediate between Gerald and the miners as the vehicles of mutual destructiveness. That the miners finally accept the machines betokens not only their nihilistic submissiveness but the deflection of their desire for violence into a quiet passion of self-destruction: Beldover, we remember, is like a town of the dead.[19]

Daleski is focusing here entirely on pre-war industrial society. But doesn't the language he uses connect almost automatically with the experience of war?

Miners with owner, circa. 1890
'in Christ he was one with his workmen . . .'
Women in Love, XVII.287

Headstocks, East Midlands coalfield
'a productive spinning, a productive repetition through eternity . . .'
Women in Love, XVII.301

DISCUSSION

'Mutual destructiveness, nihilistic submissiveness, passion of self-destruction, town of the dead'. Such terms surely belong to the experience of 1914–16? Daleski sees 'The Industrial Magnate' as the focus of a general interpretation of history offered in terms of a universal desire for violence or self-destruction. Each area of society – Shortlands, Breadalby, the Café Pompadour – is obsessed by the same lust for violent disintegration and self-destruction. Elsewhere he makes explicit the link with the war:

> The rage to destroy and to be destroyed, which, – in small compass – is present in the café, is of course the sort of rage which, intensified by public sanction, is given free rein in war; war is the ultimate consummation which the state of being of most of the characters in *Women in Love* would seem to require.[20]

The idea is in fact Lawrence's own: the chief obstacle of disagreement between himself and other anti-war intellectuals such as Bertrand Russell, was Lawrence's insistence on explaining the war, not in economic or political terms, but in terms of a psychological crisis in the human will:

> The war is dreadful. It is the business of the artist to follow it home to the heart of the individual fighters – not to talk in armies and nations and numbers – but to track it home – home – their war – and it's at the bottom of almost every Englishman's heart – the war – the desire of war – the *will* to war – and at the bottom of every German's.[21]

And in a preface to some of the poems he wrote during the war, Lawrence provided us with hints towards a theoretical method for connecting text and history:

> It seems to me that no poetry, not even the best, should be judged as if it existed in the absolute, in the vacuum of the absolute. Even the best poetry, when it is at all personal, needs the penumbra of its own time and place and circumstance to make it full and whole . . . So one would like to ask the reader . . . to fill in the background . . . with the place, the time, the circumstance. What was uttered in the cruel spring of 1917 should not be dislocated and heard as if sounding out of the void.[22]

Again, Daleski's account subtly preserves intact the novel's integrity: though the will to destruction and self-destruction exemplified by Gerald and acquiesced in by the miners is *analogous* to the will to war, war itself is only 'required', not addressed; to pursue the analogy to its conclusion would demand a different fictional situation. Lawrence's observation seems rather different in intention: he suggests that a text should be read in context, with the 'time, place, circumstance' filled in: that the reader's mind should be dispersed over the circumambient historical context rather than concentrated only on the 'dislocated' utterance. This view can be taken further: we can propose that Lawrence's vision of the perfected social machine driven by its own destructive internal contradictions is at one and the same time an interpretation of the process of industrial development *and* an interpretation of the war. Just as the violent destructiveness of Gerald's perfected machine is contained by its perfect mechanical unity, so, Lawrence argued.

> The great war does not alter our civilization one iota, in its total nature. The form, the whole form, remains intact. Only inside the complete envelope we writhe with sensational experiences of death, hurt, horror, reduction.[23]

The violence and destructiveness of war concealed itself in an ideology of 'duty' and 'honour', 'defence' and 'liberation'. Just so, Lawrence felt, the violence and destructiveness of capitalism was concealed in an ideology of productivity and democracy. Furthermore, the war was a product of the capitalist system, the violence and destructiveness of that system patently disclosed. By excluding the war from the novel, Lawrence was able to interrogate the ideology of liberal-democratic capitalism, which sustained both the system and the war:

> . . . It would be true to say that the object of the prose is at least as much the absent subject, the war, as the present subject, the mining industry (symbolizing industrial capitalism in general): a mechanical organization which combines perfect order with complete destructiveness, and which incorporates into itself, by means of their willing subjection, those whose lives are most destroyed by it. The miners who accepted the industrial and bureaucratic modernization of their industry, and the soldiers who voluntarily enlisted and marched willingly to the living death of the Western Front, become almost indistinguishable here.[24]

Compare this passage from *Women in Love* about Gerald's employees, with an extract from one of Lawrence's letters describing Cornish conscripts in 1916.

> But they submitted to it all. The joy went out of their lives, the hope seemed to perish as they became more and more mechanized. And yet they accepted the new conditions. They even got a further satisfaction out of them . . . Their hearts died within them, but their souls were satisfied.   (XVIII.304)

> Yet I liked the men. They all seemed so *decent*. And yet they all seemed as if they had *chosen wrong*. it was the underlying sense of disaster

that overwhelmed me. They are all so brave, to suffer, but none of them brave enough, to reject suffering. They are all so noble, to accept sorrow and hurt, but they can none of them demand happiness. Their manliness all lies in accepting calmly this death, this loss of their integrity.[25]

What links the two passages?

DISCUSSION

Surely what relates the two passages is Lawrence's emphasis on the passivity and submissiveness of miners and recruits: the great betrayal in each case is their *acquiescence* in the process of their own destruction. Clearly Lawrence saw both submissions as akin and of equal gravity. From a historical perspective his interpretation of the development of industrial society, particularly the mining industry, is very much open to question. The industry, which between 1905 and 1914 was being modernized in the dominant and directing hands of private ownership, was in 1915 taken into government control. From 1918 onwards the owners were faced with unrelenting demands from the workers for nationalization, a goal eventually achieved some quarter-century later. After the war, wage reductions were fought in a six-month strike, and in 1926 the resistance of the miners precipitated the General Strike.[26] The dispute of 1984–5 could perhaps be taken as an indication of the extent to which the miners have 'submitted'.

If the passage from the novel is taken in context with the letter and read as an oblique comment on the war, some of these historical difficulties disappear. All the evidence of home-front anti-war movements, conscientious objection, mutiny of troops and private resistance couldn't obliterate the massive acquiescence of millions in a futile ritual of slaughter and destruction. If Lawrence's elegy on the loss of human integrity is read as a vision of the war as well as an interpretation of industrial society, it can be seen as infinitely more convincing.

If Daleski's view, or the rather different argument I have proposed, can be accepted, Lawrence's novel is brought closer to historiography than was admitted by any of the critics mentioned earlier (above, p. 113–14). The idea that the First World War grew out of industrial capitalist society is not the only interpretation of its causes (others are mentioned in 'Further Reading') but it is certainly paralleled by the Marxist view of the war as a major transitional stage in world capitalism, a consequence of the economic crises and competing imperialist ambitions endemic to capitalism as a system:

The period of industrial capitalism was, in the main, a period of 'free competition'; a period of relatively smooth evolution and expansion of capitalism throughout the whole world, when the as yet unoccupied colonies were being divided up and conquered by armed force; a period of continuous growth of the inherent contradictions of capitalism, the burden of which fell mainly upon the systematically plundered, crushed and oppressed colonial periphery.

Towards the beginning of the twentieth century, this period was replaced by the period of imperialism, during which capitalism developed spasmodically and conflictingly; free competition rapidly gave away to monopoly, the previously 'available' colonial lands were all divided up, and the struggle for a redistribution of colonies and spheres of influence inevitably began to assume primarily the form of a struggle by force of arms.[27]

Please read Chapter XXVI ('A Chair'), especially pp. 450–2; Chapter XXIX, ('Continental'), especially pp. 478–82; and Chapter XXXI ('Exeunt'), especially pp. 578–83. Consider the following questions.

1   What meaning is attached to the 'chair' of the chapter-heading? How do you understand the role of the couple to whom the chair is presented? Do Ursula and Birkin resolve their problem in this chapter?

2   The voyage to Europe is described as 'a final transit out of life' (XXIX.479). Is that how the reader responds to this account? Is that absolute aspiration qualified in any way?

3   How does the final chapter deal with the problem of isolation and belonging?

4   To what extent can the preceding discussion of the war and Lawrence's view of modern society elucidate these passages?

(The passage in Chapter XXIX refers back to places, people and events which are to be found in the account of Ursula's early life in *The Rainbow*. A similar passage appears later in the same chapter, pp. 501–2.)

DISCUSSIONS

1   The central motif of the chair defines the theme of this chapter. Initially an object of aesthetic appreciation, the chair becomes a symbol of conventional marriage – houses, furniture, possessions, are all condemned by Birkin as 'terms of an old base world, a detestable society of man' (XXVI.445). 'One should never have a home', he says to Gerald (XXV.439); any stability or permanence of domestic living

(even the possession of a chair) seems an intolerable compromise with corrupt social institutions. The renunciation of the chair is decisively made: though some of the difficulties implicit in this position are foregrounded:

> She stood in the street contemplating.
> 'And are we never to have a complete place of our own – never a home?' she said.
> 'Pray God, in this world, no', he answered.
> 'But there's only this world,' she objected.
> He spread out his hands with a gesture of indifference. (XXVI.445).

In their pursuit of pure freedom, Birkin and Ursula pass the chair to a young working-class couple who are evidently 'having to' get married. In one sense they are offering a generous gift; in another, liberating themselves by helping to shackle others with the 'possessions' they believe to be a 'tyranny' (444). The male partner of the proletarian couple is evidently very much an inhabitant of the 'river of dissolution'; but the description of him is no simple moral rejection:

> He was a still, mindless creature, hardly a man at all, a creature that the towns have produced, strangely pure-bred and fine in one sense, furtive, quick, subtle. His lashes were dark and long and fine over his eyes, that had no mind in them, only a dreadful kind of subject, inward consciousness, glazed and dark. His dark brows and all his lines, were finely drawn. He would be a dreadful, but wonderful lover to a woman, so marvellously contributed. His legs would be marvellously subtle and alive, under the shapeless trousers, he had some of the fineness and stillness and silkiness of a dark-eyed, silent rat.
> Ursula had apprehended him with a fine *frisson* of attraction. (XXVI.446)

The language operates again by juxtaposing contrasting sensations and associations: beauty and ugliness, pleasure and distaste. 'Still, pure-bred, fine, quick, subtle, wonderful, marvellously contributed, alive, stillness, dark-eyed' are partially descriptive of one who is also 'mindless, hardly a man, a creature, furtive, dreadful'; a 'silent rat' with a 'dreadful kind of subject, inward consciousness'. Ursula's attraction towards him is like Gudrun's for the miners in Chapter IX ('Coal-Dust;') (see above, pp. 54–5).

Though Ursula finds the man appealing, and Birkin is able by a kind of mimicry to establish a 'freemasonry' with him (XXVI.447), their subsequent moral evaluation of the couple is stark in its simplicity:

> 'Children of men', he said. 'They remind me of Jesus': "The meek shall inherit the earth".'
> . . . 'And are they going to inherit the earth?' she said.
> 'Yes, they.'
> 'Then what are we going to do? she asked. 'We're not like them – are we? we're not the meek?'
> 'No. – We've got to live in the chinks they leave us'.   (XXVI.450)

Both Birkin and Ursula agree on judging the working-class couple as representative types of their society, expressing in themselves the process of disintegration and putrescence which that society is undergoing. The town seems like 'a vision of hell'; 'crowded, and like the end of the world' (450). Confronted with this prospect, both are united in their desire to be 'disinherited', to contract out of the common world and seek an alternative by directionless voyaging: 'And we will wander about on the face of the earth' (XXVI.451).

Immediately that decision has been confirmed, however, the narrative starts to raise another set of problems. Birkin and Ursula are not as harmoniously unanimous as they seem: they evidently have different conceptions of the ideal future. Ursula wants an exclusive shared freedom; Birkin a 'further fellowship':

> '. . . we want other people with us, don't we?'
> 'Why should we?' she asked.
> 'I don't know', he said uneasily. 'One has a hankering after a sort of further fellowship'.   (XXVI.451)

Though the individual liberation from society is seen as desirable and necessary, Birkin is unwilling to acquiesce in the implicit consequence of total isolation: the achieved equilibrium of heterosexual marriage is not for him an adequate basis for fulfilled living. What he wants in addition is an 'ultimate relationship' (XXVI.452) with Gerald; though Ursula condemns this as a residual will on Birkin's part to save the world by forcing people to love. 'Why can't you be single by yourself, as you are always saying? . . . [Birkin:] 'It's the problem I can't solve'. (XXVI.452)

2   The account in Chapter XXIX ('Continental'), pp. 478–82, of their travelling to Europe in a cross-channel ferry, again juxtaposes the contradictory impulses of utopian longing and sceptical resignation. Lawrence concentrates on the experience of voyaging itself, since it is there that utopian aspiration can be formulated at its most intense, before the disillusionment of arrival, the hostile reality of another confrontation with the old, ruined world, interposes between desire and its fulfilment. Birkin and Ursula experience in different ways a rapture of absolute departure; both feel they are genuinely accomplishing a 'final transit out of life' (XXIX.479). She

is lost in a delirium of hope, he in a transcendent intoxication of
'trajectory' (479). They return, of course, to the real world.

> This was the world again. It was not the bliss of her heart, nor the
> peace of his. It was the superficial unreal world of fact. Yet not quite
> the old world. For the peace and the bliss in their hearts was endur-
> ing. (XXIX.480).

The detachment of the individual from history seems complete – 'the
child she had been . . . was a little creature of history, not really herself' (XXIX.482). Yet the transformed world of the liberated consciousness endures the recurrent shock of encounter with the old,
untransformed world of reality, and has to extrapolate its utopian
longings into a tentative dimension of hope: provisional, conditional, and unrealized:

> No new earth had come to pass . . . Oh, if he were the world as well,
> if only the world were he! If only he could call a world into being, that
> should be their own world! (XXIX.482).

The issue is problematized again in a conversation, later in this same
chapter, between Gudrun and Ursula: in which Gudrun plausibly
denounces what she sees as the delusion of non-social living: 'the
only thing to do with the world, is to see it through', (XXIX.533–5).
3   The death of Gerald (to be discussed below pp. 125–6) is an
action of finality and completeness: it brings a world to an end.
Birkin stands as survivor to the tragedy, conscious of his own failure
to redeem Gerald. At the same time, Gerald has pursued his fate to an
appropriate conclusion: he has accomplished one form of apocalyptic revelation, fulfilled a 'mystery of ice-destructive knowledge,
snow-abstract annihilation' (XIX.331). Birkin's faith rests on the
eternal possibility of finding a way out, detaching the individual from
the historical process. Contemplating the cul-de-sac in which his
friend accomplished 'death by perfect cold', Birkin is unsure whether
there is any escape:

> Gerald might have found this rope . . . he might have gone on down the
> steep, steep fall of the south side, down into the dark valley with its
> pines, on to the great Imperial road leading south to Italy.
>   He might! And what then? The Imperial Road! The South? Italy?
> What then? Was it a way out? – It was only a way in again.
> (XXXI.579–80)

Birkin finds it necessary to seek consolation in contemplating a universal evolutionary mystery capable of creating beyond and after
the extinction of humanity (XXXI.580). The creative mystery can
dispense with man: so Birkin imaginatively annihilates himself in

the act of fashioning a vision of non-human development. There seems little to choose, in the end, between Gerald's heroic pursuit of death, and Birkin's imaginative commitment to the death of humanity.

The novel thus draws to its close in despair and disaster, contemplating visions of the world's end. Ultimately, however, it refuses to endorse such closure, and leaves us with Birkin and Ursula still disagreeing over the same issue: should they rest content with the exclusive intimacy of a perfected relation between themselves? Or seek for a further fellowship, strive to extend the instinct of community towards other individuals, in the hope of incorporating them into the nucleus of a new, creative society?

> 'You can't have it, because it's wrong, impossible', she said.
> 'I don't believe that', he answered.   (XXXI.583)

4   The war is surely a necessary context without which much of this novel would be difficult to understand and hard to interpret. The implicit presence of the war gives substance to Lawrence's chiliastic and prophetic preoccupations, which we might otherwise attribute to the author's paranoia or to the murky apocalypticism of his religious background and beliefs. The war can help to explain the extremity of the characters' despair and misanthropy, the intensity of their conviction that self-destruction or escapism are the only available alternatives for living in their time. It explains the isolation of those characters who survive the tragedy, their apparent helplessness and impotence. It explains the contradictory co-existence of a moral will to communicate and assist humanity, with a nihilistic impulse to renounce humanity to its self-destruction. While writing the novel in 1915 Lawrence despaired of his human audience:

> One goes on writing – to the unseen witnesses.[28]

And yet the 'Foreword' he published with the novel in 1920 contains a refutation of that displaced colloquy with the invisible:

> Men must speak out to one another.[29]

As *Women in Love* closes with Gerald's death, which is very clearly the effective collapse of Birkin's hopes for 'further fellowship', and perhaps even the destruction of an ideology or social system, as well as the death of a man, it seems appropriate to term it a tragedy. That term is highly problematical, and has been used in many different ways to different purposes (see 'Further Reading' for some of them). The simplest definition is that of a literary or dramatic work structured on the central motif of a significant death (or disaster, as tragedy need not contain a literal death). Lawrence developed several different theories of tragedy, usually specific to the nature of the work he had in hand. Read this example of one such theory, written in 1920 and referring to the labour struggles of the post-war period:

> Granted that men are still men, Labour vs Capitalism is a tragic struggle. If men are no more than implements, it is non-tragic and merely disastrous . . . If we really could know what we were fighting for, then the struggle might have dignity, beauty, satisfaction for us. If it were a profound struggle that we were convinced would bring us to a new freedom, a new life, then it would be a creative activity, a creative activity in which death is a climax in the progression towards new being.
>
> Therefore, if we could but comprehend or feel the tragedy in the great labour struggle, the intrinsic tragedy of having to pass through death to birth, our souls would still know some happiness, the very happiness of creative suffering. Instead of which we pile accident on accident, we tear the fabric of our existence fibre by fibre, we confidently look forward to the time when the whole great structure will come down on our heads . . . The essence of tragedy, which is creative crisis, is that a man should go through with his fate . . . And the whole business of life, at the great critical periods of mankind, is that men should accept and be at one with their tragedy.[30]

Lawrence distinguishes 'tragedy' from 'disaster' or 'accident': tragedy is 'creative crisis', the living through of some great cataclysm as a route to 'new life'; a death which has to be passed through to reach birth. Lawrence argued that class-conflict such as that visible in post-war Britain was not tragic, only a mechanical and material struggle without meaning or purpose. Only the awareness of 'ultimate purpose' can confer on experience the 'dignity, beauty, satisfaction', proper to tragedy.

Read the passages describing the death of Gerald, *Women in Love*, XXX–XXXI, pp. 573–83. Do Lawrence's thoughts on tragedy throw any light on this part of the novel?

DISCUSSION

As far as Birkin is concerned, at least, Gerald's death is remarkable for the absence of 'dignity, beauty, satisfaction'. It is a 'barren tragedy', devoid of ultimate meaning: Gerald's body is 'the frozen carcase of a dead male . . . a dead mass of maleness . . . cold, mute Matter' (XXXI.577–82). Birkin asserts that the friendship he offered would, if accepted, have changed the significance of his death: 'If he had kept true to that clasp, death would not have mattered'. If Gerald had struggled with Birkin in friendship (as they struggled together in

'Gladiatorial') his death could have achieved 'beauty, dignity, satisfaction': could have been more than a merely material struggle ending in wasteful death.

Birkin's affirmations here are statements of faith, and they may well seem weak when confronted with the powerful inevitability, the aesthetic finality of Gerald's death, which enacts a very old tragic form. It is at one and the same time the death of an individual, the collapse of a social system into self-destructive violence (the war), the symbolic annihilation of the white races into eternal cold, the mythological death of some pagan divinity such as Dionysos (VIII.159). Against the aesthetic weight of this complex denouement, there is nothing stronger than Birkin's clasp of hands: just as, Lawrence felt, the immense futility and agony of the war was opposed only by isolated voices speaking inwardly to 'unseen witnesses'.

> It is not Gerald's failure, though Birkin seems to think it is. The individual cannot, alone, insert those values into the social struggle by an act of will ... Birkin, the individual, proved powerless to help Gerald, because Gerald's tragedy was not an individual but a social one, and Birkin has renounced all responsibility to society. His final affirmation is an assertion of faith in 'unseen witnesses': if man has reached his cul-de-sac, his death in the snow valley, then there can only be faith in the capacity of some divine 'creative mystery', to evolve another species. Contemplating Gerald's tragic end, Birkin displays his own impotence by seeking for positive faith only beyond the society which he and the novel firmly believe is finished.[31]

Women in Love is more than a tragedy. Birkin and Ursula survive the final collapse of Gerald's world. Apocalyptic vision is accomplished by a restless, interrogating scepticism which continues to modify the stark simplicities of prophetic and tragic forms. The pressure of both apocalypse and tragedy is to close the fictional world: but *Women in Love* remains stubbornly, resolutely open, refusing to endorse the finality of closure.

Both apocalyptic and tragic theories have something in common with much of the criticism we've addressed in these pages; a theoretical premiss, central to much traditional literary criticism: that a successful work of literature must be demonstrably a coherently unified and integrated organic whole. A novel should contain great complexity of experience and a constant interaction of varied artistic ideas: but these should ultimately be subordinated or reconciled within a comprehensive totality of design. If a novel appears incomplete or contradictory, such evidence is referred as a charge of failure to some ideal norm or model of a perfectly achieved work of art.

In the last decade, literary theoreticians working within the intellectual framework of structuralist and Marxist ideas began to question this tenet of critical practice, and developed arguments for recognizing the concept of 'organic form' as a principle of bourgeois ideology. The view that fiction should present a model of organic totality was identified as a cultural equivalent of nineteenth-century bourgeois ideology's search for 'organic' concepts of society: images of the 'body politic' which would ratify it as a complex living organism, obscure the actual cultural and social contradictions of class society, and insist on the necessity of gradualist 'organic' development in preference to violent revolutionary change. Terry Eagleton in his influential book *Criticism and Ideology*, based on the theoretical work of French intellectuals such as Louis Althusser and Pierre Macherey, commented on

> ... bourgeois ideology's growing dependence on 'organicist' concepts of society. As Victorian capitalism assumes increasingly corporate forms, it turns to the social and aesthetic organicism of the Romantic-humanist tradition, discovering in art models of totality and affectivity relevant to its ideological requirements. During the second half of the century, the initially poetic notion of 'organic form' becomes progressively extended to the dominant literary mode of the time, fiction.[32]

Pursuing this relationship between fiction and ideology, literary theory discovered that the apparently perfect, seamless unities of the novel form claim an illusory integrity, analogous to the way in which social ideologies inculcate concepts of harmonious totality to conceal and mystify historical discord and contradiction. In practice works of fiction are never complete, self-sufficient and organic wholes; they are on the contrary radically incomplete, internally dissonant and self-divided. These qualities are not to be regretted or condemned, evidence that the works in question have failed to represent the world with fidelity, accuracy and truth. If novels *did* provide images of class societies as unified organic wholes they would not be representing history at all, but only articulating ideology. The usefulness of fiction is precisely its ability to subvert ideology by both expressing and interrogating it: to clarify the internal self-divisions of a novel is to bring the ideology it 'works on' under the contemplation of a critical consciousness. Louis Althusser defined the process thus:

> What art makes us *see* . . . is the ideology from which it is born, in which it bathes, from which it detaches itself as art, and to which it *alludes* . . . Novels . . . make us 'perceive' (but not know) in some sense *from the inside* the very ideology in which they are held.[33]

Fiction thus never separates itself completely from ideology, but is not on the other hand a mere expression of it: it reflects on ideology, reacts against it, puts it to work:

> The distance which separates the work from ideology embodies itself in the internal distance which, so to speak, separates the work from itself, forces it into a ceaseless difference and division of meanings. In putting ideology to work, the text necessarily illuminates the absences, and begins to 'make speak' the silences, of that ideology.[34]

We have considered extensively the work of critics who base their readings on the concept of 'organic form': in the light of this post-structuralist Marxist theory such criticism is more ideological than fiction itself, since it works to privilege organic completeness in works of art, suppresses works that don't display such integrity, reproves and corrects imbalances and distortions in the structure or body of the text. Criticism should be concerned rather to assist fiction in its natural task of illuminating and interrogating ideology. Our readings of the text of *Women in Love* have revealed considerable contradiction, self-division, fracturing and contortion of meaning within the novel's form. And Lawrence's assertion in his 'Foreword' that the war is both absent and present in the text is precisely the kind of self-division or contradiction that post-structuralist criticism is concerned to disclose. Criticism can legitimately concern itself with what a novel *excludes* from its imaginative world, as well as with what it incorporates: criticism should not *assist* the text to achieve its false ideological coherence, but should rather deny that completeness, insist on the work's partiality and limitation, its self-contradictariness and internal dissonance:

> We must not falter at the prospect of revealing formlessness in the work – as long as these words are not taken in a negative and pejorative sense. Rather than that *sufficiency*, that ideal consistency, we must stress that determinate insufficiency, that incompleteness which actually shapes the work. The work must be incomplete in itself: not extrinsically, in a fashion that could be completed to 'realize' the work. It must be emphasized that this incompleteness, betokened by the confrontation of separate meanings, is the true *reason* for its composition.[35]

'To know the work' writes Macherey 'we must move outside it'.[36] To know *Women in Love* the reader must be prepared to move outside it, to investigate its exclusions and suppressions, to recognize it as an incomplete, fragmentary component of a culture in deep crisis.

Notes

Chapter 1: Character, Narrative (pages 1–21)

1 F. Swinnerton: in *Manchester Guardian*, 15.7.1921, p. 5.
2 *Saturday Westminster Gazette*, 2.7.1921, pp. 14–15.
3 John Middleton Murry: 'The Nostalgia of Mr D. H. Lawrence', *Nation and Athenaeum*, 13.8.1921; also in Murry: *Reminiscences of D. H. Lawrence*, (Cape, 1933). Quoted in Colin Clarke (ed.): *'The Rainbow' and 'Women in Love': A Selection of Critical Essays*, (Macmillan, 1969), p. 68.
4 F. R. Leavis: *D. H. Lawrence* (Cambridge Minority Press, 1930), pp. 10–11.
5 E. Shanks: in *London Mercury* (August, 1921), p. 433.
6 W. C. Pilley: in *John Bull* (17.9.1921), p. 4.
7 George J. Zytaruk and James T. Boulton (eds): *The Letters of D. H. Lawrence*, vol. II, (Cambridge University Press, 1981), pp. 182–4. Letter of 5.6.1914. The Futurists were a group of artists who advocated taking industrial machinery as a subject: see the notes on this in the Cambridge *Letters*; and compare the sculptor Loerke, *Women in Love* (XXIX.517–19).
8 Aldous Huxley: 'Introduction' to *The Letters of D. H. Lawrence* (Heinemann, 1932), pp. xxi–xxiii.
9 H. M. Daleski: *The Forked Flame* (Faber, 1965), 76–7.
10 Julian Moynahan: *The Deed of Life* (Princeton University Press, 1963), pp. 40–2.
11 *Letters*, I, p. 477. Letter of 19.11.1912.

Chapter 2: Ideas, Language pages 21–42)

1 D. H. Lawrence: *Fantasia of the Unconscious* (Heinemann, 1923), pp. 14–15, 74, 64–5.
2 F. R. Leavis: *D. H. Lawrence: Novelist* (Chatto and Windus, 1955), p. 183; 'That Birkin is substantially Lawrence there can be little temptation to deny . . .'
3 *Letters*, II. pp. 468–9. Letter of 7.12.1915.
4 *Letters*, I. p. 503. Letter of 17.1.1913.

5   Graham Hough: *The Dark Sun* (Duckworth, 1956), p. 86.
6   Leavis, Op. Cit. (1955), p. 213.
7   D. H. Lawrence: 'The Novel', in *Phoenix II*, ed. Warren Roberts and Harry T. Moore (Heinemann, 1968).
8   *Letters*, II, p. 275. Letter of 3.8.1915.
9   *Letters*, II, p. 650. Letter of 4.9.1916.
10 Leavis, Op. Cit. (1955), p. 184..
11 Terry Eagleton: *Exiles and Emigrés* (Chatto, 1970), pp. 208–9.
12 D. H. Lawrence: 'Foreword' to *Women in Love* (1920). See Clarke: *Critical Essays* (1969), p. 64.
13 Leavis, Op. Cit. (1955), pp.154–4.
14 Derek Bickerton: 'The Language of *Women in Love*' in *A Review of English Literature*, VIII, ii. (1967), pp. 56–67.
15 Ian Robinson: 'D. H. Lawrence and English Prose', in Andor Gomme (ed.): *D. H. Lawrence: A Critical Study of the Major Novels and Other Writings* (Harvester, 1978), pp. 15–16. Robinson is actually discussing *The Rainbow*.

Chapter 3: Creativity, Dissolution (pages 43–62)

1   F. R. Leavis: *Thought, Words and Creativity: Art and Thought in Lawrence* (Chatto, 1976). For Leavis (1930), see Chapter 1, note 4.
2   Leavis, Op. Cit. (1955), p. 152.
3   Ibid., p. 164.
4   Ibid., p. 182.
5   Ibid., p. 162.
6   Colin Clarke: 'Introduction' to Clarke: *Critical Essays* (1969).
7   Ibid., p. 10.
8   *Fleurs du Mal* (flowers of evil) was the title of a volume of verse by the French 'decadent' poet Charles Baudelaire. (1821–67)
9   Catherine Carswell: *The Savage Pilgrimage* (Chatto, 1932), pp. 68–9.
10 D. H. Lawrence: 'The Reality of Peace', in Warren Roberts and Harry T. Moore (ed.): *Phoenix II* (Heinemann, 1968).
11 Keith Sagar: *The Art of D. H. Lawrence* (Cambridge University Press, 1966), pp. 83–4. See p. vii for acknowledgement of the debt to Leavis. See also George Ford: *Double Measure: A Study of the Novels and Stories of D. H. Lawrence* (Holt, Rinehart & Winston, 1965), p. 168; and *River of Dissolution* (Colin Clarke: 1969), pp. x–xi.
12 Sagar, Op. Cit. (1966), pp. 82–3.
13 Clarke: *River of Dissolution*, pp. 75–6.
14 Sagar, Op. Cit. (1966), p. 83.
15 Leavis, Op. Cit. (1976), p. 86.
16 See Stephen Miko: *Toward Women in Love* (Yale University Press, 1972), p. 242.
17 F. R. Leavis, 'The Orthodoxy of Enlightenment' in *'Anna Karenina' and Other Essays* (Chatto, 1967).

Chapter 4: Sexual Politics: Homosexuality, Feminism (pages 62–82)

1   George Eliot: *Felix Holt the Radical* (1867), Ch.1.

2 Terry Eagleton: *Literary Theory: An Introduction* (Blackwell, 1983), p. 215.
3 Kate Millett: *Sexual Politics* (Hart-Davis, 1971; Virago, 1977), p. 239.
4 Ross 'Introduction' to *Women in Love*, (Penguin English Library, 1982), pp. 30–1.
5 Julian Moynahan, Op. Cit. (1963), p. 63.
6 Middleton Murry in Clarke: *Critical Essays* (1969), p. 84.
7 George Ford (1965), in Clarke: *Critical Essays* (1969), p. 84.
8 Kermode in Clarke: *Critical Essays* (1969), p. 216. See Ch. 5, p. 15.
9 *Letters*, II. p. 115. Letter of 2.12.1913.
10 *Letters*, II, p. 320. Letter of 19.4.1915.
11 '"Prologue" to *Women in Love*', in Clarke: *Critical Essays* (1969), pp. 57–61.
12 Quoted by George H. Ford: 'Introductory Note to Lawrence's "Prologue" to *Women in Love*', *Texas Quarterly*, VI, (1963); in Clarke: *Critical Essays* (1969), p. 40.
13 Ibid., p. 41.
14 Hilary Simpson: *D. H. Lawrence and Feminism* (Croom Helm, 1982), p. 13.
15 J. Middleton Murry: *Son of Woman* (Cape, 1931), p. 72.
16 Norman Mailer: *The Prisoner of Sex* (Sphere, 1972), p. 133.
17 Lydia Blanchard: 'Love and Power: a Reconsideration of Sexual Politics in D. H. Lawrence', *Modern Fiction Studies*, 21, (1975), pp. 431–2.
18 Kate Millett, Op. Cit. (1971), pp. 262–4.

Chapter 5: Metaphysic, Apocalyse (pages 82–101)

1 Clarke: *Critical Essays* (1969), p. 17.
2 See 'Further Reading' under *Modernism*.
3 Hough, Op. Cit. (1956), p. 79.
4 Leavis, Op. Cit. (1955), p. 87.
5 Mark Kinkead-Weekes: 'The Marble and the Statue: the Exploratory Imagination of D. H. Lawrence', in Maynard Mack and Ian Gregor (eds): *Imagined Worlds: Essays in Honour of John Butt* (Methuen, 1968), p. 411.
6 Clarke: *River of Dissolution* (1969), p. 100.
7 Kinkead-Weekes in Mack and Gregor, Op. Cit. (1968), pp. 410–11.
8 'The Crown' and 'The Reality of Peace' in *Phoenix II* (1968).
9 'Study of Thomas Hardy' in Edward D. McDonald (ed.): *Phoenix; the Posthumous Papers of D. H. Lawrence* (Heinemann, 1936).
10 Letters, II. p. 212. Letter of 5.9.1914.
11 Letters, II. pp. 137–8. Letter of 19.1.1914.
12 *Phoenix* (1936), p. 419.
13 Kinkead-Weekes in Mack and Gregor, Op. Cit. (1968), p. 380.
14 Letters, II, p. 390. Letter of 11.9.1915.
15 Frank Kermode: 'Lawrence and the Apocalyptic Types', *Critical Quarterly*, X, (1968); reprinted in Clarke (ed.): *Critical Essays* (1969). Quotations from Clarke, p. 208.
16 See Letters, II, p. 669. Letter of 31.10.1916.

17   Particularly by Frank Kermode: *Lawrence* (Fontana, 1973), pp. 68–9; and Op. Cit. in Clarke: *Critical Essays* (1969).
18   See for example D. H. Lawrence: *'Apocalypse' and Other Writings on Revelation,* ed. Maria Kalnins, (Cambridge University Press, 1980); and 'Hymns in a Man's Life' in *Phoenix II* (1968).
19   See Kermode, Op. Cit. (1969, 1973).
20   Letters, II, p. 424. Letter of 2.11.1915.
21   Letters, II, p. 528. Letter of 7.2.1915.
22   Letters, III, pp. 142–3. Letter of 27.7.1917.
23   See Kermode, Op. Cit. (1973), pp. 68–9.
24   See Kermode in Clarke: *Critical Essays* (1969), pp. 216–7.
25   Middleton Murry in Clarke: *Critical Essays* (1969), p. 71.
26   Kermode, Op. Cit. (1973), p. 73.
27   See above, Chapter Three, p. 49–52.
28   Clarke: *River of Dissolution* (1969), pp. 37–8.
29   See Leavis, Op. Cit. (1955), p. 154–5.

Chapter 6: Biography, History (pages 102–128)

1   Letters, II, p. 528. Letter of 7.2.1916.
2   See 'Review' of *Georgian Poetry 1911–12,* in Anthony Beal (ed.): *Selected Literary Criticism of D. H. Lawrence* (Heinemann, 1956).
3   See D. G. Wright: 'The Great War, Government Propaganda and English "Men of Letters", 1914–16,' *Literature and History,* 7, (1978).
4   See Paul Delaney: *D. H. Lawrence's Nightmare,* (Harvester, 1979), Ch. III.
5   See Bertrand Russell: 'Philosophy of Social Reconstruction', in Harry T. Moore (ed.): *D. H. Lawrence's Letters to Bertrand Russell* (New York, 1948). See Letters, II, p. 378–81. Letter of 16.8.1915.
6   See D. H. Lawrence: *Twilight in Italy* (written 1912/3) (Heinemann, 1956), Ch. II.
7   See Raymond Williams: *Culture and Society 1780–1950* (Chatto, 1958; Penguin, 1961) for a history of this tradition.
8   Letters, II, p. 339. Letter of 14.5.1915.
9   Letters, II, p. 331. Letter of 30.4.1915. See also Chapter Two above, p. 00.
10 *Letters,* II, pp. 285–6, Letter of 12.2.1915.
11 Graham Holderness: *D. H. Lawrence: History, Ideology and Fiction,* (Gill and Macmillan, 1982), p. 200. Quotation from Lawrence in *Letters,* II, p. 593. Letter of 7.4.1916.
12 'Foreword' to *Women in Love* (1920), in Clarke: *Critical Essays* (1969), pp. 63–4.
13 Leavis, Op. Cit. (1955), p. 32.
14 Holderness, Op. Cit. (1982), p. 200.
15 Daleski, Op. Cit. (1965), p. 127.
16 Leavis, Op. Cit. (1955), p. 110.
17 John Worthen: *D. H. Lawrence and the Idea of the Novel,* (Macmillan, 1979, pp. 98–9.
18 David Craig: *The Real Foundations: Literature and Social Change* (Chatto, 1973), pp. 143–4.

19 Daleski, Op. Cit. (1965), p. 147.
20 Ibid., p. 135.
21 Letters, II, p. 233. Letter of 18.11.1914.
22 D. H. Lawrence: 'Note' to *Rhyming Poems*; in *Complete Poems*, I, (Heinemann, 1957), pp. xxxvi–xxxvii.
23 *Phoenix II*, pp. 207–8.
24 Holderness, Op. Cit. (1982), pp. 207–8.
25 *Letters*, II, p. 625. Letter of 9.7.1916.
26 Lawrence's own reaction to the 1926 strike was recorded in 'Return to Bestwood', (written in 1926), in *Phoenix II* (1968).
27 J. Stalin: 'The Programme of the Communist International', in Emile Burns, (ed.) *A Handbook of Marxism* (1937), p. 967.
28 *Letters*, II, p. 602. Letter of 1.5.1916.
29 Lawrence: 'Foreword', in Clarke: *Critical Essays*, (1969), p. 64.
30 Lawrence: 'Preface' to *Touch and Go*, (1921); in *Phoenix*, (1936), p. 291.
31 Holderness, Op. Cit. (1982), pp. 217–8.
32 Terry Eagleton: *Criticism and Ideology*, (Verso, 1978), p. 103.
33 Louis Althusser: *Lenin and Philosophy* (trans. Ben Brewster, New Left Books, 1971), pp. 203–4.
34 Eagleton, Op. Cit. (1978), p. 89.
35 Pierre Macherey: *Towards a Theory of Literary Production* (trans. Geoffrey Wall, Routledge and Kegan Paul, 1978), p. 79.
36 Ibid., p. 132.

Suggestions for Further Reading

Ideally, a 'Further Reading List' (or, more forbiddingly, a 'Select Bibliography') should be the beginning of a student's independent work on a text, author or period. The *Guide* has made extensive use of critical writing on D. H. Lawrence; but as the use of criticism is often specific to a particular point, you won't get from the *Guide* itself much idea of how that critic addresses other problems, or literature in general. Furthermore, a *Guide* to a specific text can't give to the larger general issues it must inevitably raise the attention they require: you will need, in other words, to go yourself directly to works of criticism and theory in order to absorb and evaluate their contributions to our understanding of the text in question and of literature as a whole.

   The list that follows is not a comprehensive bibliography of writing on *Women in Love*, and certainly not an adequate summary of general works available. It is designed rather to guide you into criticism and theory by presenting a selection of what seem to me the most useful titles, and giving you some idea of their character and value. Only a few titles on larger topics are included: but these works, where indicated, contain their own comprehensive bibliographies on the subjects they address.

Chapter 1

Lawrence's revolutionary theory of 'character' is discussed in most of the standard critical works, but especially Moynahan (1963) and Daleski (1965). The most interesting recent book on theories of character is Jeremy Hawthorn: *Multiple Personality and the Disintegration of Literary Character* (Edward Arnold, 1983). The texts documenting Lawrence's own theories of fiction are usefully collected in Anthony Beal (ed.): *Selected Literary Criticism of D. H. Lawrence* (Heinemann, 1956); and the theories themselves are addressed by Gamini Salgado in the *London Magazine, 7*, (1960); and by D. J. Gordon in *D. H. Lawrence as a Literary Critic* (New Haven: Yale University Press, 1966). Mary Freeman studied the impact of Futurist ideas in 'Lawrence and Futurism' in Clarke (ed.): *Critical Essays* (1969). A substantial body of material exists on the Freudian background: the German intellectual context is thoroughly documented by Martin Green in *The von Richthofen Sisters* (Weidenfeld and Nicolson, 1974); the influence of Freudian thinking on Lawrence is treated in D. A. Weiss: *Oedipus in Nottingham* (Seattle: University of Washington Press, 1962) and in F. J. Hoffmann: 'Freudianism and the Literary Mind' in Harry T. Moore and F. J. Hoffmann (eds): *The Achievement of D. H. Lawrence* (Norman: University of Oklahoma Press, 1953); and a very accomplished Freudian literary-critical approach to Lawrence can be found in Dorothy van Ghent: *The English Novel, Form and Function* (Rinehart, 1953; Harper, 1961).

Two articles on narrative are worth consulting, though neither deals specifically with *Women in Love*: Roger Sale: 'The Narrative Technique of *The Rainbow*', in *Modern Fiction Studies*, v, (1959); and S. L. Goldberg: '*The Rainbow*: "Fiddlebow and Sand"', in *Essays in Criticism*, XI, no. 4, (1966). The most useful modern book on narrative is Shlomoth Rimmon-Kenan: *Narrative Fiction: Contemporary Poetics* (Methuen, 1983), which also has an excellent bibliography. Reviews and other evidence about contemporary reception of *Women in Love* can be found in R. P. Draper (ed.): *D. H. Lawrence: the Critical Heritage* (Routledge and Kegan Paul, 1970), and in W. T. Andrews (ed.): *Critics on D. H. Lawrence* (Allen and Unwin, 1971).

Chapter 2

The best exploration of *Women in Love* in terms of its containment of ideas is F. H. Langham: '*Women in Love*', in Andrews (ed., 1971). Traditional literary criticism has tended to set up the relationship between literature and 'ideas' as a series of oppositions: between 'experience' and 'intellect', the 'concrete' of literature and the 'abstract' of ideas. A useful focus of the traditionally 'empiricist' approach to the problem is F. R. Leavis: 'Literary Criticism and Philosophy', *Scrutiny*, 5, (1937); also in *The Common Pursuit*, (Chatto and Windus, 1952; Penguin, 1962). American 'New Criticism' of the 1950s banished ideas from literature altogether: you would find a theoretical statement of this position in W. K. Wimsatt and Monroe C. Beardsley: *The Verbal Icon* (Methuen, 1970); and a Marxist critique of 'New Criticism' in Jeremy Hawthorn: *Identity and Relationship* (Lawrence and Wishart, 1973). More recently, the whole debate has been absorbed into the broader question of literature's relationship with *ideology*: influential criticism based largely in French theoretical work has shown that criticism, by its very denial of ideas, is adopting a specific position within *ideology*. The best introduction to this current of thought is Terry Eagleton: *Criticism and Ideology* (Verso, 1976); and the ideological character and context of *Women in Love* are addressed in Holderness (1982).

Roger Dataller looks at Lawrence's use of language in 'Elements of

D. H. Lawrence's Prose Style', in Andrews (ed., 1971). David Lodge's *The Language of Fiction* (Routledge and Kegan Paul, 1966) is a useful general book on language in novels. The best recent study of language as a specific critical approach to fiction is Roger Fowler: *Linguistics and the Novel* (Methuen, 1970), which has an excellent bibliography of works on linguistics, linguistic criticism, structuralist analysis of narrative and theory of fiction.

Chapter 3

The relationship between Lawrence's fiction and the criticism of Leavis is documented (from a partisan position) in P. J. M. Robertson: *The Leavises on Fiction* (Macmillan, 1981). The significance of Leavis' criticism in its general cultural context is subjected to penetrating critical analysis in Perry Anderson: 'Components of the National Culture', *New Left Review*, 56, (1968); Raymond Williams: 'Sociology and Literature', *NLR*, 67, (1971); Terry Eagleton: *Literary Theory: an Introduction*, (Blackwell, 1983) and *The Function of Criticism* (Verso, 1984). Mark Spilka demonstrates the influence of Leavis on Lawrence criticism in 'Post-Leavis Lawrence Critics', *Modern Language Quarterly*, 25, (1964). Kingsley Widmer's *The Art of Perversity* (Seattle: University of Washington Press, 1962) is a useful complement to Colin Clarke's *River of Dissolution* (1969). Lawrence's Romantic ancestry is addressed in Herbert Lindenberger: 'D. H. Lawrence and the Romantic Tradition', in Harry T. Moore (ed.): *A D. H. Lawrence Miscellany*, (Carbondale: Southern Illinois University Press, 1959). The cultural influences which form the background to Colin Clarke's study can be traced in Mario Praz: *The Romantic Agony* (trans. Angus Davidson, 2nd ed., Oxford University Press, 1951); Richard Gilman: *Decadence* (Secker and Warburg, 1975); and in Holderness (1982).

Chapter 4

Other feminist approaches to Lawrence can be found in Anne Smith (ed.): *Lawrence and Women* (Vision, 1978); and Carol Dix: *D. H. Lawrence and Women* (Macmillan, 1980). Germaine Greer's *The Female Eunuch* (St Alban's: Paladin, 1971) examines literature generally from a feminist perspective; and an up-to-date general study can be found in Toril Moi: *Sexual/Textual Politics* (Methuen, 1985). G. Wilson Knight: 'Lawrence, Joyce and Powys', *Essays in Criticism*, XI, no. 4, (1962), discusses the anal sexuality of relationships in the novel.

Chapter 5

Lawrence's 'apocalyptic' writings are collected and surveyed in Mara Kalnins (ed.): *D. H. Lawrence: Apocalypse and the Writings on Revelation* (Cambridge University Press, 1980). T. A. Smiles examines the novel as 'myth' in 'The Mythical Bases of *Women in Love*', *D. H. Lawrence Review*, I, (1968); and J. B. Vickery takes the same approach in his *Myth and*

Literature (Lincoln, Nebraska, 1966). Angelo P. Bertocci addresses the novel rather as 'symbolism' in Moore (ed., 1959). The *D. H. Lawrence Review*, 2, (1969) contains two discussions of Lawrence's 'war essays': R. D. Beards: 'Lawrence and the *Study of Thomas Hardy*', and M. Beker: '*The Crown, The Reality of Peace* and *Women in Love*', a broader study of Lawrence's Utopian perspective can be found in E. Goodheart: *The Utopian Vision of D. H. Lawrence* (Chicago: University of Chicago Press, 1963). Peter Faulkner: *Modernism* (Methuen, 1977) is a good short introduction to the cultural changes of the period.

Chapter 6

At present the standard biography of Lawrence is Harry T. Moore: *The Priest of Love* (Heinemann, 1974); though Keith Sagar's *D. H. Lawrence: Life Into Art*, (Viking, Penguin, 1985) is more recent. These works will be superseded by a three-volume biography in preparation by Cambridge University Press. Edward Nehls: *D. H. Lawrence: a Composite Biography* (especially vol. I, 1885–1919) is a fascinating collage of biographical material (Madison: University of Wisconsin Press, 1957).

Scott Sanders: *D. H. Lawrence: the World of his Major Novels* (Vision, 1973), is a good historical analysis; and C. P. Griffin: 'The Social Origins of D. H. Lawrence', *Literature and History*, 7:2, (1981) an important up-dating of evidence. The historical context itself can be introduced by three works: G. C. H. Whitelock: *250 Years in Coal* (Nottingham: privately, 1947) documents local conditions by tracing the history of the Barber-Walker dynasty, models for the coal-owning Crich family in *Women in Love*; A. R. Griffin: *Mining in the East Midlands* (Frank Cass, 1971) fills in the broader social and economic context; and Eric Hobsbawm's *Industry and Empire* (Weidenfeld and Nicolson, 1968; Penguin, 1969) supplies a general historical contextualization. Other approaches to the *causes* of the war can be found in A. J. P. Taylor: *The First World War* (1963).

Specific evidence and discussion of Lawrence's war experiences can be found in Harry T. Moore: *D. H. Lawrence's Letters to Bertrand Russell* (New York: Gotham Book Mart, 1948); in Bertrand Russell's *Portraits from Memory* (Allen & Unwin, 1958); and in N. Myers: 'Lawrence and the War', *Criticism*, 4, (1962). Delaney (1979) is the fullest treatment.

D. J. Gordon examines Lawrence's relationship with tragedy in 'Lawrence's Quarrel with Tragedy', *Perspective*, 13, (1964); and there is a brilliant discussion of the same topic in Raymond Williams: *Modern Tragedy* (Chatto and Windus, 1966).

If you are interested in pursuing the critical approaches sketched in the closing pages of Chapter Six, you should begin with Althusser (1971), Macherey (1978) and Eagleton (1976, 1983, 1984). Graham Martin discusses the problems of class in Lawrence's work in 'D. H. Lawrence and Class', in Douglas Jefferson (et. al., eds.), *The Uses of Fiction: Essays in Honour of Arnold Kettle*, (Open University Press, 1982). A video film drawing on Eagleton (1976) and Holderness (1982) studies Lawrence in his historical context: *D. H. Lawrence and The Culture Industry,* prod. 'Red Dirt' for the Alternative Video Group (1985).

Index